Tainted Love

Tainted Love

From Nina Simone to Kendrick Lamar

Alex Coles

Sternberg Press

For Sophie

Soft Cell's version of the Northern soul song that *Tainted Love: From Nina Simone to Kendrick Lamar* is affectionately named after was a UK number one hit in 1981 and today has over half a billion streams on Spotify. The band's vocalist, Marc Almond, aptly refers to Soft Cell's song as a "three-minute piece of twisted pop perfection."[1]

"Tainted Love" is just one example of a tainted love song. The other songs included in *Tainted Love* tilt toward other genres and eras, and vary widely in terms of the types of taint they describe. What they share is a tendency to define themselves in contrast to other types of ballads. In this sense, where the love song simply says, "I love you," and the torch song pleads, "I love you, don't leave me," the tainted love song admits, "I love you, but in an unusual way."

In contrast to its vernacular use, in popular music a taint is never pejorative. A taint can be overt, as per Soft Cell's queering of "Tainted Love" or the fetishism explored by Roxy Music's 1973 ode to a blow-up doll, "In Every Dream Home a Heartache." A taint can just as readily be the way feelings of confusion, grief, or inferiority are expressed. Realized through a play of voices projecting contrasting narratives, Kendrick Lamar's 2017 "LOVE." explores feelings of acute insecurity. Released decades after Roxy Music's and Soft Cell's tracks, dealing with a less blatant taint, and from within a very different genre, "LOVE." is a more subtle tainted love song.

The songs explored in *Tainted Love* each represent the respective musicians' creative peak. Declaring love for his recently murdered songwriting partner, with "Here Today" Paul McCartney composes a love song from a position of grief arguably stronger than the many other love songs populating his back catalogue.

The precise taint of each of the songs is emphasized through a particular sonic technique. Triggered by North American imperialism at the time of the Cold War, and responding to Latin American feelings of inferiority based on their economic status as a "Third World" region, the plaintive lyrics of Antonio Carlos Jobim and Frank Sinatra's 1969 rendition of "Off Key" sit uneasily on a bed of instrumental and vocal dissonance. For Jobim, inferiority is the taint and dissonance the sonic key. The poignant lyrics of Joni Mitchell's 1971 "All I Want," essaying the singer's frustration at the restrictive role society placed on women at the time, are delivered using vocal and instrumental subtlety. For Mitchell, frustration is the taint and subtlety the sonic key.

Setting frequently informs a song's taintedness. This is present in Soft Cell's "Tainted Love" in the form of the band's camp styling, fed in from London's and New York's gay club scenes. By contrast, the context of Nina Simone's 1978 version of "Baltimore"—the Civil Rights era and the decay of North American inner cities—informs her empathic lament.

The tainted love song brazenly stretches out across boundaries of genre. *Tainted Love* moves fluidly from alternative rock with the Velvet Underground in 1968, bossa nova with Jobim a year later, folk with

Mitchell in 1971, art rock with Roxy Music in the early 1970s, reggae with Simone in 1978, pop with McCartney in 1982, and electro-pop with Soft Cell and Charlotte and Serge Gainsbourg in the early 1980s. The trajectory moves back to alternative rock with PJ Harvey and Nick Cave's murder ballad of the mid-1990s and fast-forwards to hip-hop with Lamar in 2017 and post-grime with Little Simz today. Tainted love songs continue to hold sway, irrespective of genre, generation, or gender.

1. Marc Almond, *Tainted Life* (London: Pan Books, 2000), 111.

I

Kendrick Lamar, "LOVE." (2017)

Insecurity

Divided between lyrics pledging romantic love and
those pleading for its reciprocation, Kendrick Lamar's
"LOVE." is a penetrating exploration of emotional
insecurity. The insecurity Lamar conveys is enhanced
by an urgent demand for his love's confirmation.
Lamar's acute emotional intelligence transforms
"LOVE." from a standard love song into a tainted one.
   Lamar's willingness to embrace contradiction

lends his track a certain believable gravitas. In the song, various characters give alternative accounts of the same story. Different voices articulate these contrasting points of view, presenting opposing versions of a narrative simultaneously. "I've always been heavy on vocal tone," explains Lamar, as "different tones [...] give off a different expression."[1] Indeed, the albums Lamar has released show a constant experimentation with vocal tone.[2] This can vary dramatically from one track to another but also from one word to the next. On verses in "Backseat Freestyle," from *good kid, m.A.A.d city* (2012), Lamar strains his voice for emphasis on the word "dream." On "Untitled 02 | 06.23.2014.," from *untitled unmastered.* (2016), Lamar grinds out a coarse vocal that lifts into a higher range with the last word of each line for emphasis. On "LOVE.," from *DAMN.* (2017), Lamar crafts a tone that is comparatively warm and gentle—appropriate for a romantic ballad, even a tainted one.

One of the musicians Lamar frequently name-checks, and who stresses the counterpoint between love and insecurity using nuance in vocal tone, is Marvin Gaye. That Gaye achieves this by coining some of the most infectious rhythms of the era only adds to their potency. Two romantic ballads from *Let's Get It On* (1973) explore love and insecurity respectively: on "If I Should Die Tonight" Gaye pledges love, while "Please Stay (Once You Go Away)" reflects on loss. In both tracks, Gaye uses different voices simultaneously.[3] "Overdubbing those voices—stacking the vocals—was a technique he mastered," recalls one studio observer, and "each of these voices was unique—a sweet falsetto, a tender midrange, a sexual growl, a bottommost plea."[4] Unlike Lamar, Gaye does not use these multifarious voices as a way to provide contrasting points of view in the same song; rather, narrative tracks are kept quite separate and singularity is the key.

As one of the most sympathetic interpreters of other songwriters' articulations of love and insecurity in the early '70s, Donny Hathaway moved freely between soul and rock sources. By covering Gaye's "What's Going On" and John Lennon's "Jealous Guy" on *Live* (1972), Hathaway highlights the close correspondence— in treatment of emotive subject matter if not in style—between Gaye and Lennon as contemporary musicians of different genres.[5] After all, *What's Going On* and *Imagine* (the LP with "Jealous Guy") were both released in 1971.

Like Gaye, Lennon approaches love and jealousy in a disarmingly direct way. "Jealous Guy" seeps insecurity, including the lines "I was feeling insecure / You might not love me anymore." Footage of the recording of the vocals for "Jealous Guy" reveals the delicate emotional shading Lennon was capable of achieving: as the word "insecure" is sung, Lennon drags it out—the emphasis increasing the weight of the word, pushing its emotive potential. For once, the double tracking plaguing so many of his vocals (Lennon was notoriously insecure about his voice) is eschewed. Unlike much of Lennon's output, a startingly naked single-track vocal performance is all that was used in the final mix. More than any other musician of his generation, Lennon could identify fundamental human emotions lyrically and then transmit them vocally with incredible precision. "Jealous Guy" is a vital precedent when considering "LOVE."

In contrast to Lennon's and Gaye's songs covered by Hathaway, "LOVE." encompasses duality both lyrically and vocally. To allow different vocal textures to communicate the thoughts of opposing characters, Lamar features guest vocalists. Lyrically, the questions propelling the verses forward almost chastise the partner they are aimed at—as if probing each aspect of a relationship to ensure the foundations underpinning it are sound. With the line "If I didn't ride blade on curb, would you still (love me)?" Lamar tests whether a partner's love is predicated on him having a successful music career. But the last two words of the phrase are delivered by Zacari, whose voice, treated with what sounds like auto-tune, lifts into the falsetto range. Zacari also later repeats the couplet, but not in falsetto: "Give me a run for my money / There is nobody, no one to outrun me." Cutting across this, Lamar's baritone repeats the phrase "I wanna be with you, ay." The line seems to bounce across the melodic scale, ending on the low note sounded by the "ay." Together, Zacari's and Lamar's voices envelope the listener in a cascading play of textures, the contrast between them running parallel with the one between love and insecurity. Unusually, the typical tonal roles are inverted, as the baritone delivers lyrics describing insecurity and the falsetto those pledging love.

The effect of Zacari's and Lamar's voices together is akin to Prince's solo voice on the song "The Beautiful Ones," ranging from falsetto on the line "Baby, baby, baby," all the way down to baritone with the couplet "Don't make we waste my time / Don't make me lose my mind, baby." On the latter, Prince throws his voice to such a degree the effect is vertiginous, the listener feeling as if they're actually riding the emotional rollercoaster being described in the lyrics. Lamar underlines Prince's importance in terms of variance of vocal tone: "[the contrast

between Prince's] falsetto [and] his baritone [...]
gave you so many different emotions."[6] Lamar brings
in Zacari as a guest vocalist as if to achieve the vocal
range he associates with Prince.

The composition of a hip-hop track is typically
a collaborative process, with one musician providing
the beat, another the hook, and the primary rapper
often penning the bulk of the lyrics. Zacari also
collaborated on the composition of "LOVE." Lamar's
own version of the compositional process emphasizes
that no matter how complex the collaborative process
is, the song is simply a vehicle for delivering emotion:

> we get in the studio and I can go off a simple drum
> loop that I like. My process, it starts from a whole
> bunch of premeditated thoughts: the process of
> me thinking about the ideas and what I want to say
> next. By the time I get into the studio I have to find
> that exact sound that triggered the emotion or idea
> that I thought about two months ago. [...] And I
> have to remember these things. I have to write them
> down and then months later I have to find that same
> emotion that I felt when I was inspired by it. I have
> to dig all the way deep to see what were the things
> that triggered the ideas.[7]

The asynchronous nature of the songwriting process
permeates the finished track—the verses of "LOVE."
tend not to segue smoothly into one another. On
first listen, the varying texture of the voices in the
different sections makes it feel like the components
are almost arbitrarily spliced together. This sense
of discontinuity is set against a beat and backing
that initially serves to provide the only elements of
continuity the song appears to have. The push and pull

between these extremes lend the track a tension that makes it addictive, as with each repeated listen, the various sections start to run together more smoothly.

The duality of narratives and vocal textures held in tension on "LOVE." is complemented by a similar approach to instrumentation. This sensibility derives from Lamar's attraction to jazz fusion, particularly Herbie Hancock's *Head Hunters* (1973) and Miles Davis's *On the Corner* (1972), LPs on which rock and funk were first incorporated into jazz. "I was in the studio one day," explains Lamar, "Terrace Martin [the producer of *To Pimp a Butterfly*] noticed something about the type of sounds [... and] instruments that I was picking and was like: 'man, a lot of the chords that you pick are jazz influenced. You are a jazz musician by default with the way your cadence is rapping over a certain type of snare and drums.'"[8] The exchange between hip-hop and jazz fusion piloted by A Tribe Called Quest's debut album, *People's Instinctive Travels and the Paths of Rhythm* (1990), soon led to Q-Tip's production of tracks such as Nas's "One Love" on *Illmatic* (1993). With this history in mind, Lamar's *To Pimp a Butterfly* features arrangements by saxophonist Kamasi Washington, bassist Thundercat, and keyboardist Robert Glasper, lending the instrumentation a complex jazz-derived rhythmic basis over which the various vocal tones float.[9] After *To Pimp a Butterfly*, the impact of jazz fusion becomes less explicit with *DAMN.* and *Mr. Morale & The Big Steppers* (2022), but its principles continue to inform many of Lamar's vocal and instrumental decisions. Jazz fusion allows Lamar to instrumentally access duality, especially on "LOVE."

The insecurity running through "LOVE." opens to other emotions triggered by unease and vulnerability.

Depression persists as a theme throughout Lamar's writing, beginning with his track "Mortal Man" on *To Pimp a Butterfly*: "I remember you was conflicted / Misusing your influence / Sometimes I did the same / Abusing my power, full of resentment / Resentment that turned into a deep depression." In an interview, Lamar refers to the tension that arises from the tendency toward duality underpinning much of his work: "The kid in me, the person who never had nothing growing up is saying, 'I want to spend this shit on some chains and a car' [and ...] the side that's on the records is telling me, 'You need to think wisely.' I've been conflicted like that since I was a little boy. Doing music is the only way for me to get that conflict out."[10] By riding duality, "LOVE." works through the conflict first set out on "Mortal Man."

The specific duality explored in "LOVE." underpins Lamar's broader approach of constantly trafficking between the social and the individual. This differentiates Lamar from two of the historical figures mentioned earlier. Where Gaye devoted an LP to the social (*What's Going On*), his subsequent album dealt with the personal (*Let's Get It On*). The pattern of Lennon's releases at the time was similar, with the shift from *Imagine* to *Some Time in New York City* (1972). Over four decades later, Lamar embraces duality, pursuing both the personal and political simultaneously — not only on the same LP but in the very same song. Exploration of the social is rooted in the individual and vice versa.

The contradictions Lamar explores through lyrics and vocal tone are augmented by the ample interpretative room given to the listener, allowing them to establish their own rapport with the feelings and scenarios being described. "I know it'll be challenging for a listener," Lamar comments, referring to the lyrical and instrumental duality structuring many of his tracks, "[but] the process of me making [music] is the same process the listener's going to have to deal with."[11] That the listener seems to be a consideration during the composition process indicates both the openness and the complexity of Lamar's songwriting. "This is the challenge for me: being able to talk about anything and make a connect to a listener, where a listener can either feel like you or feel like they understand you."[12] Imagining the listener's response to this degree allows Lamar to optimize his impact on them—appropriate given how love songs are frequently addressed to a "you." Whether empathizing with Lamar's bold expressions of love, the tortuous feelings of insecurity, or his tendency to ricochet between the two, the listener is folded into his tainted love song.

1. Kendrick Lamar, "Kendrick Lamar Meets Rick Rubin and They Have an Epic Conversation," interview by Rick Rubin, *GQ*, October 20, 2016, https://www.youtube.com/watch?v=4lPD5PtqMiE.

2. See Nina Sun Eidsheim, *The Race of Sound: Listening, Timbre, and Vocality in African American Music* (Durham, NC: Duke University Press, 2019).

3. See Andrew Flory, "Marvin Gaye as Vocal Composer," in *Sounding Out Pop: Analytical Essays in Popular Music*, ed. John Covach and Mark Spicer (Ann Arbor: University of Michigan Press, 2010), 63–98.

4. Quoted in Jan Gaye, *After the Dance: My Life with Marvin Gaye* (New York: Amistad, 2013), 52.

5. For an in-depth analysis, see Emily J. Lordi, *Donny Hathaway Live* (London: Bloomsbury, 2016).

6. Lamar, "Kendrick Lamar Meets Rick Rubin."

7. Lamar, "Kendrick Lamar Meets Rick Rubin."

8. Lamar, "Kendrick Lamar Meets Rick Rubin."

9. See Sequoia Maner, *To Pimp a Butterfly* (London: Bloomsbury, 2022).

10. Kendrick Lamar, quoted in "Kendrick Lamar: 'I Am Trayvon Martin. I'm All of These Kids,'" interview by Dorian Lynskey, *Guardian*, June 21, 2015, https://www.theguardian.com/music/2015/jun/21/kendrick-lamar-interview-to-pimp-a-butterfly-trayvon-martin.

11. Lamar, quoted in "Kendrick Lamar: 'I Am Trayvon Martin.'"

12. Lamar, "Kendrick Lamar Meets Rick Rubin."

2

Nina Simone, "Baltimore" (1978)

Empathy

"Baltimore" is unique in this book for being one of only two songs included that was not composed by its performer. Where Randy Newman's original 1977 recording is a dispassionate comment on Baltimore, Nina Simone's version from a year later infuses the song with a heightened degree of emotional empathy. Simone's "Baltimore" is a paean to a city with deep personal and political significance. "Nina had a way

of taking a piece of music and not interpreting it,"
says Simone's long-term guitarist Al Schackman,
but "morphing it into her own experience."[1] This is
precisely what Simone does on "Baltimore," turning it
into a love song to a city experiencing rapid, racialized
socioeconomic decline. Simone introduces an abrupt
change in vocal texture at a crucial moment in the
song's chorus—a technique the singer refers to as a
"razor cut"—to convey her empathy with the plight
of the city.[2] This move is the key sonic element that
turns this love song into a tainted love song.

For a portion of the decade preceding "Baltimore,"
Simone's oeuvre had oscillated between love
songs and protest songs, a movement crucial to
understanding the significance of her version
of "Baltimore." Released in 1964, "Mississippi
Goddam" is Simone's first overt protest song,
written in response to the death of four young African
American girls from a white supremacist's bomb
in September 1963. "The entire direction of my life
[then] shifted," Simone explains, "and for the next
seven years I was driven by civil rights and the hope
of black revolution."[3] Composed two years later,
"Four Women" "capsules completely the problem
of the blacks in America among the women," explains
Simone.[4] In 1968, she releases "Why? (The King of
Love is Dead)"—a passionate eulogy to Martin Luther
King, Jr., first performed days after his assassination.
Accounting for this gradual shift away from love songs
toward protest songs, Simone commented: "I stopped
singing love songs because my protest songs were
needed. So the direction I'll take in the future depends
entirely on what happens to my people. If my people
go back into hiding, perhaps I'll start singing love
songs again."[5]

"Baltimore" is an exception, since the subtly of Simone's performance demonstrates how a protest song and a love song need not be mutually exclusive. "There's a song I sing called 'Baltimore,'" comments Simone in an interview, "and it directly refers to 'See the little seagull, trying to find the ocean, looking everywhere.'"[6] The next verse depicts people "Drunk lyin' on the sidewalk / Sleepin' in the rain," while another describes how the city's inhabitants hide their faces and their eyes "Cause the city's dyin' / And they don't know why." By dropping the *g*'s and reducing vibrato, Simone emphasizes the harshness of the images. When it finally comes, the chorus provides a distinct point of contrast with the verses. With less words per line, Simone's voice is free to sound out each one more fully. "Oh, Baltimore," Simone sings, "Man, it's hard just to live." Stretching the word "hard" by breaking it up so it's phrased as "ha-r-r-r-d," Simone conveys a succinct sense of empathy.

Simone explains that the verse following the chorus "refers to [how] I'm going to buy a fleet of Cadillacs and take my little sister, Frances, and my brother, and take them to the mountain and never come back here, until the day I die. When I went to Africa, I thought that I would be taking them with me."[7] Simone lived in Liberia from 1974 to 1977, just prior to moving her home to Paris and recording "Baltimore" in Brussels in January 1978. Revealing the degree of her investment in the city, Simone personalizes "Baltimore" implicitly in the studio recording by contrasting the delivery of the verse with the chorus, and explicitly when performing it live or commenting on it in interviews.

Simone's notion of the razor cut is crucial to the way "Baltimore" works as a tainted love song,

25

a technique she piloted on "Four Women" (which was sampled in 2017 by Jay-Z on "The Story of O.J."). The song describes four women, opening with a detailed account of the first one, Aunt Sarah. "My skin is black / My arms are long / My hair is woolly," sings Simone in a deep, thick voice. Named Saffronia and Sweet Thing, the second and third women are, respectively, tan and yellow. With lyrics telling how "My manner is tough / I'll kill the first mother I see," the listener expects an appropriately aggressive name to be assigned to the song's final character. Confounding the listener's expectations, Simone pauses and fiercely pronounces her name is "Peaches"—a name evoking softness and sweetness. "All my songs, the important ones, have razor cuts," explains Simone, "I cut you, I make you think and it's immediate."[8] Unlike in "Four Women," where the razor cut comes with the very last word, in "Baltimore" Simone makes her move between the verse and chorus. The initial verses detail the city's struggles, and the listener expects the chorus to continue in this vein. Instead, the way Simone delivers the lines "Oh, Baltimore / Man it's ha-r-r-r-d just to live" is significantly different, full of compassion. The listener doesn't expect this degree of empathy after the piercing observations in the verses.

At the time of writing the song, Randy Newman had never visited Baltimore; his song about the city was written from a comfortable distance in Los Angeles. Hailing from the same LA singer-songwriter scene of the late '60s as Joni Mitchell, Newman's singing, like his lyrics to "Baltimore," sounds singularly unemotive, sardonic even. Newman feels closer to songwriters like Leonard Bernstein, whose city-themed songs ("New York, New York" from the play *On the Town* [1949]) were fused with emotion by the likes of Frank Sinatra and Billie Holiday. This tradition of interpretation contributes to Simone's license to use and make Newman's lyrics her own. Newman's comments on "Baltimore" reveal the level of technical precision involved in his crafting of the song's lyrics and their meter. "The 'beat up little seagull' [line] always bothered me," says Newman, as "[it's] a little long, but it's obviously setting a scene."[9] Newman wrote the song while looking at pictures of Baltimore from *National Geographic*, inspiring the vignettes sketched in the verses. That Newman had established no personal connection with the city at the time of writing the song is evident in his performance.

In contrast to Newman, Simone's empathy for Baltimore is (possibly) informed by an experience there a decade earlier. On the evening of February 20, 1967, Simone was preparing to go on stage at the Civic Center. By her own account, the singer was found "staring into the mirror putting make-up in my hair, brown make-up, because I wanted to be the same color all over."[10] More disturbing, Simone explains, were the "visions of laser beams and heaven" from the same episode.[11] A harbinger of forthcoming battles with mental health, the hallucinations were partly the result of fatigue from overwork. This episode remained so lucid that Simone could recount it in detail decades later.

Following the riots after King's murder in April 1968—an event leading to Simone's LP *'Nuff Said* the same year—Baltimore's economic decline in the face of deindustrialization accelerated as both local and federal government failed to provide sufficient aid. Knowing this lends Simone's delivery of lines like "'Cause the city's dyin'" additional poignance. If Simone's own experience there in 1967 informs how the singer turns "Baltimore" into a love song, the way it dovetails with the city's harsh socioeconomic predicament in 1978 also makes it a protest song.

The decision to record "Baltimore" for jazz fusion label CTI Records rests with label owner Creed Taylor, who attended Simone's concert in London in September 1977. A reviewer of the concert notes how "[Simone] was giving of herself more openly, more deeply, than most artists I've ever seen. And the overwhelming impression was one of simmering anger born of a multitude of pains and sorrows, personal grief and universal injustice."[12] Simone brings this arsenal of emotions to "Baltimore," the recording of which was first broached by Taylor the night of the London concert. In an interview, Taylor recalls the difficulties involved in recording in Brussels's Studio Katy in January 1978, with an uncooperative Simone frequently arguing with the musicians.[13] To guitarist Eric Gale's attempts to find a reggae pulse for "Baltimore" in the studio, Simone responded, "what is this corny stuff?"[14] Standoffs between Simone and the other musicians followed. At one point during the recording sessions, Taylor recalls Simone becoming particularly difficult, the singer and producer eventually going for a walk on the terrace outside the studio to clear the air. Evidently, Taylor felt it worth persevering as "the beauty of Nina's voice is that you believe what she sang."[15]

Simone may have complained in her autobiography about not personally choosing "Baltimore," but her reservations about the reggae treatment adopted by the session guitarist Gale implies she didn't fully appreciate the sensitivity of his playing.[16] Fresh from jamming with musicians in Jamaica, Gale had recently appeared on Roberta Flack's *Killing Me Softly* (1973) and Esther Phillips's *Capricorn Princess* (1976), making the guitarist an apt choice. Simone's reservations also suggest an indifference to the political significance of reggae in the late '70s—both Peter Tosh's *Equal Rights* and Bob Marley's *Exodus* were released in 1977, a year before Simone's "Baltimore." So convincing was Simone's reggae treatment that on hearing it, the Jamaican band the Tamlins cut a version with Sly Dunbar and Robbie Shakespeare in 1979.

Vocally, "Baltimore" benefits from the change in Simone's voice over a decade earlier, when it became a richer instrument, full of dark shadings. "Mom said that her voice broke," explains her daughter, "and that if you listen to her songs, there was pre-getting mad and post-getting mad. She's singing love songs, and her voice and her approach is much lighter. And then from 'Mississippi Goddam' in 1964 on, it was as if her voice just dropped, and it never returned to its former octave."[17] This newfound depth allows Simone to infuse lyrics with gravity, as if her voice literally increases in weight. In Liz Garbus's 2015 documentary *What Happened, Miss Simone?*, Simone reflects on this: "What I was interested in was conveying an emotional message, which meant using everything you've got inside you sometimes to barely make a note. If you have to strain to sing you sing. So sometimes I sound like gravel and sometimes I sound like coffee and cream."[18] Throughout the song's verses, the "coffee and cream" end of Simone's vocal range reigns, but when the word "ha-r-r-r-d" is phrased in the chorus,

29

it's sung using a voice with "gravel" in it. This abrupt change in vocal texture and the way it works against the grain of the song's lyrics (it might be more obvious to use the gravel voice in the verses depicting the city's harsh conditions) makes this one of Simone's most effective razor cuts.

Emphasized by the abrupt contrast between the verse and the chorus, "Baltimore" is a love song to a city, tainted by both Simone's personal experience there and its social and economic struggles. Simone's ability to take Newman's cold social critique and turn it into a vehicle to portray Black resilience at the end of the '70s makes "Baltimore" an unlikely but enthralling tainted love song.

1. Al Schackman, quoted in Alan Light, *What Happened, Miss Simone?* (Edinburgh: Canongate, 2016), 51.

2. Nina Simone, quoted in Light, *What Happened, Miss Simone?*, 134

3. Nina Simone, *I Put a Spell on You: The Autobiography of Nina Simone* (Boston: Da Capo Press, 1991), 91.

4. Simone, quoted in Light, *What Happened, Miss Simone?*, 132.

5. Simone, quoted in Light, *What Happened, Miss Simone?*, 221.

6. Simone, quoted in Light, *What Happened, Miss Simone?*, 210.

7. Simone, quoted in Light, *What Happened, Miss Simone?*, 210.

8. Simone, quoted in Light, *What Happened, Miss Simone?*, 134.

9. Randy Newman, interview by Mark Horowitz, Library of Congress, November 11, 2013, https://www.loc.gov/item/webcast-6375.

10. Simone, *I Put a Spell on You*, 110.

11. Simone, *I Put a Spell on You*, 111.

12. Cliff White, "Nina Simone, Theatre Royal, Drury Lane, London," *New Musical Express*, December 10, 1977.

13. Marc Myers, "Nina Simone: 'Baltimore,'" *Jazz.FM91*, February 21, 2013, https://jazz.fm/nina-simone-qbaltimoreq/.

14. Nina Simone, quoted in Nadine Cohodas, *Princess Noire: The Tumultuous Reign of Nina Simone* (New York: Pantheon, 2010), 292.

15. Creed Taylor, quoted in Myers, "Nina Simone: 'Baltimore.'"

16. Simone, *I Put a Spell on You*, 167–68.

17. Lisa Simone Kelly, quoted in Light, *What Happened, Miss Simone?*, 100.

18. Nina Simone, quoted in Liz Garbus, dir., *What Happened, Miss Simone?* (Los Gatos, CA: Netflix, 2015).

3

Roxy Music, "In Every Dream Home a
Heartache" (1973)

Fetishism

The lonely protagonist of Roxy Music's "In Every
Dream Home a Heartache" is in love with an inflatable
doll. "Immortal and life size / My breath is inside you,"
sings Bryan Ferry, "I'll dress you up daily / And keep
you till death sighs." If fetishism, understood as the
association of sexual gratification with an object, is
the taint to "In Every Dream Home a Heartache," then

dissonance—lyrically, vocally, and instrumentally—
is the sonic key.

By recasting what constitutes a romantic ballad,
on "In Every Dream Home a Heartache" Roxy Music
craft an exceptionally tainted love song. Parallel with
the Velvet Underground's "The Gift" and Charlotte
and Serge Gainsbourg's "Lemon Incest," the band
overtly explore taboo through popular music. Using
humor to provoke, the typical object of heterosexual
male affection is replaced by an actual object,
a plastic doll. Is Roxy Music commenting on the
detrimental role of consumer society in producing
idealized versions of the female form? Are they
simply reinforcing a number of clichés about the
way the male gaze fetishizes aspects of women's body
and dress? Or are they doing both simultaneously?

The song begins with a series of eerie ambient
swirls made by a synthesizer, courtesy of Brian Eno,
punctuated by occasional stabs on a keyboard. Ferry
delivers the first verse using an almost unemotional,
melancholic tone. Like in a play, it acts as a comment
on the narrative about to unfold, with the protagonist
claiming, "In every dream home a heartache / And
every step I take / Takes me further from heaven."
The rest of the verse's lyrics detail how, despite the
penthouse apartment, all is not well. The first verse
ends with the lines "But what goes on? / What to do
there? / Better pray there." For the first time, there
is a flicker of emotion in Ferry's voice.

As the story unfolds, Eno's ambient swirls
gradually increase in intensity. The second verse
reveals that the narrator has acquired an inflatable
doll, with Ferry singing, "I bought you mail order /
My plain wrapper baby." The degree of fetishism
then goes up a notch as the narrator describes how

"My role is to serve you / Disposable darling," and then up another with the lines "My breath is inside you / I'll dress you up daily / And keep you till death sighs." The emphasis on breath and death pulls us deeper into the narrator's fetish.

Then everything changes as the song takes a sharp turn into total dissonance. The line "I blew up your body" is the last one delivered using the emotionless voice. By way of response, the very next line, "But you blew my mind," is sung using a voice double tracked at increased volume, lending it a cartoonish character. Phil Manzanera's guitar begins to screech and Ferry screams "In every dream home a heartache" over and over again. Personifying dissonance, Ferry develops what sounds like a cyborg croon, an effect achieved by pushing the multiple-tracked voice until it verges on the point of feedback. The synth and keyboards take turns while Paul Thompson fires off tom fills until the song seems to end. An outro repeats the last instrumental section and finally, the track is brought to a close.

As the last track on side one of *For Your Pleasure* (1973), the story of a bachelor's fetish underpinning "In Every Dream Home a Heartache" sits comfortably within the themes of the LP's songs. "The Bogus Man" is about a sexual stalker: "The bogus man is at your heels / Now clutching at your coat / You must be quick now hurry up / He's scratching at your throat." Meanwhile, "Editions of You" and "Beauty Queen" approach images of female beauty, referring to "swimming pool eyes" and "a pin-up done in shades of blue," respectively. And "Grey Lagoons" and the title track feature Ferry speaking to a presumed lover.

The key to Roxy Music's lyrical approach lies in their sources. As a student of Richard Hamilton's in the mid-'60s, Ferry was schooled in the more conceptual approach to Pop art—typified by the collage the former produced with John McHale, *Just What Is It That Makes Today's Homes So Different, So Appealing?* (1956). On multiple occasions in the '70s, Ferry draws on Hamilton, evident in the 1976 song title "This Is Tomorrow," which is borrowed from a 1953 exhibition of the same name by the Independent Group, a collective Hamilton was a part of. "I must have been thinking about Richard [Hamilton], the consumer thing," says Ferry of the lyrics of "In Every Dream Home a Heartache," as "here's a guy in the song who has everything and nothing."[1] Lyrically, Hamilton serves as a deep creative well for Ferry, with the tone and length of the title seemingly deriving from the collage *Just What Is It That Makes Today's Homes So Different, So Appealing?* Certain phrases used in the lyrics even appear as if lifted from popular magazines.

"In Every Dream Home a Heartache" draws just as much on the Pop art of Allen Jones as it does on that of Hamilton. While the difference between them is not so cut and dry, and in the mid-'60s Jones makes use of the same visual language as Hamilton, by the end of the decade Jones exclusively focuses on fetishizing the female form. Often abhorred, typical of Jones's work of the late '60s is *Table* (1969), a sculpture consisting of a model of a female figure looking very much like an inflatable doll crouching on all fours to support a glass tabletop. With *Table* Jones simultaneously reinforces and questions clichés pertaining to female sexuality. Knowing it will provoke, with "In Every Dream Home a Heartache" Ferry lyrically revisits this moment in Pop art in order to trigger the same process of questioning.

Doubling down on the questions the song asks about the idealized female form, by drawing on Jones, the album cover of *For Your Pleasure* features a picture of the model Amanda Lear wearing a tight-fitting black leather skirt. By locating a schism between these two different types of Pop art at the very heart of "In Every Dream Home a Heartache," Ferry ensures the song polarizes opinion. PJ Harvey even composed a direct comment on the song by playing up its perversity: on the 1993 track "Claudine, the Inflatable One," Harvey rasps, "Claudine, I love ya, don't be shy / Come round my place, I'll blow your mind."

This polarization is knowing. Eno, who was influenced by the music of Can, particularly Holger Czukay's use of the synthesizer, draws on their instrumentalization of dissonance. With an emphasis on improvisation and experimentation evidencing their debt to the Velvet Underground's first two albums, Can's debut LP, *Monster Movie* (1969), pursues dissonance through free jazz and psychedelic rock. Building on this, their album *Tago Mago* (1971) moves further into instrumental dissonance through the clash of polyrhythms.

Where Ferry explores dissonance lyrically and vocally, Eno confronts it through instrumentation. When the two are run together, the effect is magnified. But Ferry's more mainstream vision for Roxy Music meant only so much dissonance could be part of the band's future. Similar to Lou Reed pushing John Cale out of the Velvet Underground a few years earlier, Eno was ejected from Roxy Music. "Apart from the competition aspect," says Ferry, "I just felt that if it was going to get better [...] we had to add a more musical dimension to the band."[2] Ferry continues: "The thing with Eno came to a head during the

American tour. I just got very pissed off with reading articles supposedly pertaining to Roxy Music but in fact talking about Eno. [...] Or, later on, reading an American review of *For Your Pleasure* which stated that Eno sang lead vocals on half the tracks."[3]

While "In Every Dream Home a Heartache" probes stereotypes of femininity, crucially this tainted love song also essays the dissonance between Eno and Ferry. In this sense, the song carries a portent of an intermusical dynamic that was crucial to Roxy Music. With Eno's exit from the band, dissonance was largely eschewed and Roxy Music became more polished as the decade wore on. Parallel with the loss of dissonance, under Ferry's stewardship Roxy Music retreated from the edginess of the tainted love song toward the relative conservativism of the torch song and the love song.

1. Bryan Ferry, quoted in Nick Kent, "Bryan Ferry," *New Musical Express*, January 19, 1974.
2. Ferry, quoted in Kent, "Bryan Ferry."
3. Ferry, quoted in Kent, "Bryan Ferry."

4

Joni Mitchell, "All I Want" (1971)

Frustration

Featuring one of the most sonorous soprano vocal performances in popular music, "All I Want" arrests the listener for the duration of the song. The vocals serve the lyrics, which essay the gender-biased restrictions Joni Mitchell was encountering. "All I Want" boldly goes to the very heart of what Mitchell was looking for: the freedom to have romantic relationships, be a mother, and develop as a singer and songwriter. The restrictive era of the mid-'60s made being a single mother and performing all but impossible, and the hypocrisy of the music business in the late '60s and into the early '70s meant female musicians were criticized for exploring multiple romantic relationships. By staging the difficulties created by these circumstances, "All I Want" outlines Mitchell's predicament. "Free love—now we know there's no such thing. Pay later, always," a wizened Mitchell commented while looking back at the era.[1] Demanding freedom to love unhampered by social convention, Mitchell's "All I Want" voices an acute sense of frustration. Typical of Mitchell's complex nature, this frustration is projected via lyrical and vocal subtlety, not sonic aggression, rendering a most tender tainted love song.

"All I Want" is the first track on side one of *Blue* (1971), an LP typical of the emotive, Los Angeles singer-songwriter wave of the early '70s, sitting comfortably next to Neil Young's *After the Gold Rush* (1970) and James Taylor's *Mud Slide Slim and the Blue Horizon* (1971). Mitchell attests to feeling "like my guts were on the outside" when writing *Blue*, conveyed by the subtlety of the instrumentation and the emphasized lyrics expressing Mitchell's frustration.[2] The line "Oh, I love you when I forget about me" finds Mitchell describing the way she can only love another when denying her sense of self. More dramatic lines follow: "Do you see, do you see, do you see how you hurt me, baby? / So I hurt you too / Then we both get so blue." Struck with the word "both," the high note sustained for the rest of the line conveys sorrow. Explaining these lyrics, Mitchell comments: "In the state that I was at in my inquiry about life and direction and relationships, I perceived a lot of hate in my heart. You know, 'I hate you some, I hate you some, I love you some, I love you when I forget about me.' I perceived my inability to love at that point. And it horrified me."[3]

The dilemma Mitchell experienced by being a mother and a partner while writing and performing no doubt contributed to her self-professed "inability to love." Perhaps it was not an inability but a frustration triggered precisely by the restrictive nature of the time. Only a writer struggling against an era of conservatism and chauvinism could have penned such a moving tainted love song.

While offering a critique, the lyrics of "All I Want" simultaneously celebrate romantic relationships. When Mitchell sings, "Do you want, do you want, do you wanna dance with me, baby?" the word "wanna" is phrased using multiple notes, with the voice and lyrics working in perfect unison to communicate a sense of freedom in pursuing fresh romance. Describing the capacity to fully give oneself to another, "All I Want" includes what is arguably one of the most gushing couplets in romantic song: "I wanna talk to you, I want to shampoo you / I want to renew you again and again." The emotive power behind Mitchell's delivery of the word "shampoo" overcomes what for another songwriter would veer toward schmaltz.

Vocally, Mitchell pushes her soprano to the limit. "Miles Davis taught me how to sing," Mitchell says. "More and more I'm beginning to show what he taught me—pure straight tones holding straight lines. The feeling when you sing and you open up your heart. If you remember to keep your heart open it produces a warmer tone than if you really think you're hot shit, because the tone is going to get cold then."[4] Though perfecting a type of artifice that gives the impression of the lyrics appearing to convey direct emotion, Mitchell usurps the temptation to indulge in technical demonstrations of vocal prowess. The net result is an emotive and sophisticated vocal style.

To arrive at the technique by which lyrics address their antagonist, Mitchell purloins from the model of songwriting Bob Dylan piloted in the mid-'60s: "[Dylan's] influence was to personalize my work. I feel this for you, or from you or because of you."[5] Wanting to broach more emotional topics than Dylan in the '60s, Mitchell goes in a different direction. She explains how examining emotional relationships is crucial to her songwriting: "Love is a peculiar feeling, because it's subject to so much change. [...] I keep asking myself, 'What is it?'"[6] This open embrace of love, whether tainted or not, leads Mitchell to in turn influence Dylan. *Blood on the Tracks* (1975), an LP brimming with tainted love songs that detail the end of a marriage, would likely not have been possible without *Blue*.

Mitchell articulates her feelings of frustration by striking a balance between melody and lyrics. "The thing I was reluctant to let go of was the melodic, harmonic sense. [... With] Dylan, you could speak in paragraphs [but at] the sacrifice of music."[7] Consequently, "it was my job to distil a hybrid that allowed for a certain amount of melodic movement and harmonic movement [...] but with a certain amount of plateaus in order to make the longer [lyrical] statement."[8] With different degrees of emphasis, Mitchell's entire development as a songwriter comes down to a playoff between plateaus of lyrical narrative and melodic and harmonic movement. The playoff allows Mitchell to develop a unique sonic and lyrical dynamic, accounting for the subtlety of "All I Want."

In interviews, Mitchell openly details her attempts

at a conventional lifestyle in the mid-'60s, giving birth to a daughter in 1965 and then marrying in 1966, prior to breaking through as a songwriter in 1967. In song, Mitchell immediately acknowledges her struggles and frustrations in a more obtuse way, portraying the futility of her first marriage on "I Had a King" from 1968. Lines from "Little Green," also on *Blue*, refer to the experience of surrendering a child for adoption: "So you sign all the papers in the family name / You're sad and you're sorry, but you're not ashamed."[9] Two years later, after breaking into the music business, Mitchell was forced to face its hypocrisy. The caption to an illustration in a *Rolling Stone* article from August 1971 pathetically refers to Mitchell as the "Queen of El-Lay" by highlighting her romantic relationships with other members of the LA singer-songwriter community, but seldom questioning her male counterparts.[10]

Following *Blue*, Mitchell begins to turn away from the autobiographical, and by the time of *The Hissing of Summer Lawns* (1975), she is totally outward facing as a lyricist. "I began to write social description," Mitchell affirms, "as opposed to personal confession."[11] *The Hissing of Summer Lawns* narrates the lives of those who gave up the freedom Mitchell chose a decade earlier and instead opted for emotional security. The characters populating the LP would, in Mitchell's parlance, hang on to both their king and baby. "In *Hissing*, some women didn't like the mirror that it held up," says Mitchell, since "a lot of it was the description of the trapped housewife."[12] The bland state of satisfaction achieved by the characters referred to on the title song could not contrast more with the progressive, emotional upheaval experienced by the autobiographical narrator of *Blue*.

Included on the second volume of Mitchell's archive series in 2021, the early rendition of "All I Want" was accompanied only by a dulcimer—the first verse is simply hummed—while consecutive verses feature lyrics that are quite different to those presented in the definitive version on *Blue*. The live version of "All I Want," recorded for the BBC in October 1970, reveals Mitchell striving to go beyond the simpler lyrics associated with her most recent LP, *Ladies of the Canyon* (1970), without yet being able to achieve the lyrical complexity of *Blue*, completed a year later.

By the time Mitchell comes to record "All I Want," the instrumentation remains appropriately pared back, ensuring each subtle vocal inflection is audible. The infectious bounce of Mitchell's dulcimer is accompanied by the conga playing of Russ Kunkel— a Miles Davis band alumni—with James Taylor's acoustic guitar sweetening the bare arrangement here and there. Kunkel describes how "There was always a rhythmic template to Joni's music, and she set it. She set it with what she played, or with the cadence of what she sang, or a combination of subdividing the tempo with what she was singing and the tempo of what she was playing, and they were always well matched."[13]

The emotions explored on "All I Want" required new guitar chords and tunings, together providing the subtlety characteristic of the songs from *Blue*. "A lot of [...] my complex chords," says Mitchell, "contain emotional nuances that are forbidden within the laws of music."[14] Thereafter, as melody begins giving way to modality, lyrics are forced into a secondary role, enhanced on the jazz-inflected LPs of the late '70s. Lyrical directness only returns when Mitchell's arrangements are simplified again in response to new wave music with *Wild Things Run Fast* released in 1982.

Mitchell's tainted love song "All I Want" renders her frustration with society and the music business palpable. Yet with sonic subtlety, the song also remains optimistic in tone due to its infectious rhythm and melody.

1. Joni Mitchell, quoted in David Yaffe, *Reckless Daughter: A Portrait of Joni Mitchell* (New York: Sarah Crichton Books, 2017), 126.
2. Joni Mitchell, quoted in Joni Mitchell and Malka Marom, *Joni Mitchell: Both Sides Now* (London: Omnibus Press, 2014), 57.
3. Joni Mitchell, quoted in "Joni Mitchell: An Interview, Part Two," interview by Penny Valentine, in *Joni on Joni: Interviews and Encounters with Joni Mitchell*, ed. Susan Whitall (Chicago: Chicago Review Press, 2019), 59.
4. Mitchell, quoted in Mitchell and Marom, *Joni Mitchell*, 128.
5. Mitchell, quoted in Yaffe, *Reckless Daughter*, 46.
6. Mitchell, quoted in Mitchell and Marom, *Joni Mitchell*, 81–82.
7. Mitchell, quoted in Yaffe, *Reckless Daughter*, 46.
8. Mitchell, quoted in Yaffe, *Reckless Daughter*, 46.
9. Gabrielle Glaser refers to the "baby scoop era," whereby a child born to an unwed mother in North America was immediately taken away by an adoption agency. See Gabrielle Glaser, *American Baby: A Mother, a Child, and the Shadow History of Adoption* (London: Penguin Books, 2022).
10. Timothy Crouse, "Blue," *Rolling Stone*, August 5, 1971, https://www.rollingstone.com/music/music-album-reviews/blue-104415/.
11. Joni Mitchell, quoted in "Joni Mitchell Defends Herself," interview by Cameron Crowe, in *Joni on Joni*, 96.
12. Mitchell, quoted in Mitchell and Marom, *Joni Mitchell*, 116.
13. Russ Kunkel, quoted in Yaffe, *Reckless Daughter*, 135.
14. Mitchell, quoted in Mitchell and Marom, *Joni Mitchell*, 64.

5

The Velvet Underground, "The Gift" (1968)

Macabre

This macabre yet humorous tainted love song is
a tale of how a lovestruck student's plan to mail
himself to his girlfriend ends in tragedy. Delivered
with a distinctive Welsh lilt, John Cale's comically
understated voice never wavers, even when the gory
details of Waldo Jeffers's demise are described. If
the macabre is the theme of the Velvet Underground's
"The Gift," then repetition—of Cale's voice and the

band's crunching guitar-driven instrumental—is the sonic key. Where "the first [LP] had [...] some beauty," Cale says, the second LP with "The Gift" "was consciously anti-beauty."[1]

Composed during a period when Reed was still in college and focused on writing fiction, the narrative was inspired by his separation from a girlfriend during summer vacation. "[One] night Cale and I were sitting around and he said, 'Let's put one of those stories to music,'" recalls Reed of their conversation.[2] Cale confirms that "it was my idea to do it as a spoken word thing. We had this [...] instrumental, so instead of wasting it we decided to combine them."[3] In the finished recording, the narrative is panned to the left speaker and the instrumental to the right, allowing them to be listened to separately. "If you got tired of the words," says Reed, "you could just listen to the instrumental," and vice versa.[4] This simultaneity means the repetition taking place in each channel is obfuscated. Vitally, the separate character of the two channels—particularly the way they seem disconnected and then momentarily connected—lends the track added complexity, essential given how it lasts for over eight minutes.

The opening line of "The Gift" sets the scene: "Waldo Jeffers had reached his limit. It was now mid-August, which meant he had been separated from Marsha for more than two months." The narrative details lovesick Waldo's worries that Marsha is cheating. After checking the mailbox to see if there is a letter from Marsha, Waldo hits on an idea: Lacking the money to travel to Wisconsin, why not mail himself there? After purchasing the necessary packing material from the supermarket, Waldo surmises that "a few air holes, some water, perhaps some midnight snacks, and it would probably be as good as going tourist." The post office picks Waldo up.

The story then shifts to the receiver of the package, Marsha, casting her mind back to the previous weekend. "She had to remember not to drink like that. Bill had been nice about it though. After it was over, he'd said he still respected her." Evidently, Waldo's worst fears had come true. Her best friend Sheila Klein enters, and as they talk, Cale's voice becomes more animated. Their conversation is interrupted when the postman delivers a large package. "Ah God, it's from Waldo," exclaims Marsha. "That schmuck," replies Sheila. Attempts at opening the tightly sealed package are in vain. Remembering the tools her father kept in the basement, Marsha retrieves a large sheet metal cutter and hands it over to Sheila. After a failed attempt, Sheila says, "I got an idea... just watch," and grasping the sheet metal cutter by both handles, she plunges the blade into the package, right through Waldo's head.[5] Making light of the ghastly, the story concludes with Cale delivering a line describing how Waldo's head "split slightly and caused little rhythmic arcs of red to pulsate gently in the morning sun."

The narrative of "The Gift" holds listeners' attention with a dark humor and twisted plot, and when experienced with the instrumental, it accrues a layering beyond the irreverent. With Cale on bass, Reed on guitar, Maureen Tucker on drums, and Sterling Morrison on guitar, the band grind out the repetitive blues rock riff that drives "The Gift." The instrumental is fueled by the fuzz of the guitars, with Morrison recalling: "There was fantastic leakage 'cause everyone was playing so loud and we had so much electronic junk with us in the studio—all these fuzzers and compressors. [Engineer] Gary Kellgren, who is ultra-competent, told us repeatedly: 'You can't do it—all the needles are on red.' And so the album is fuzzy, there's all that white noise."[6]

The sound of "The Gift" was prototyped with the instrumental "Guess I'm Falling in Love," which was cut just prior to the recording of *White Light / White Heat*, in early September 1967, the band feeling rhythmically tight due to Cale switching from viola to bass to lock in with Tucker's drumming. With Cale mostly alternating between bass and keyboard on each track, the LP's sonic texture is consistent throughout. The way the spoken narrative and instrumental channels of "The Gift" interplay creates an engaging complexity. When Cale reads the part detailing Waldo's worries, the rhythmic instrumental just continues despite the emotive turn the narrative has taken. By contrast, when Cale delivers the lines about images of Marsha embracing another man permeating Waldo's thoughts, the lead guitar jumps out of the dense fuzz: Waldo's nagging paranoia seems to be literalized by the jagged lead line and the menacing feedback that follows. This guitar lick is repeated later when Cale arrives at the line where Waldo checks the mailbox, except that now the narrative and the instrumental appear totally disconnected again. Emphasizing the addition of a new character, when Sheila enters the story, Cale's bass playing becomes more prominent. Finally, a cleaner version of the circular guitar riff driving the entire track rings out after Cale has delivered the last gruesome line of the story. The way the two channels run parallel—at times seeming to interfere with one another and at others not—is crucial to the way "The Gift" stages macabre humor via repetition.

White Light / White Heat is arguably the Velvet

Underground's most cohesive and powerful LP, with each of its six tracks exploring another facet of the perverse. Side one opens with the title track, which approximates the experience of an amphetamine rush; "The Gift" is next; then "Lady Godiva's Operation" provides a horrific optic onto a sex change gone wrong; and "Here She Comes Now" focuses on the moment of female orgasm. On side two, "I Heard Her Call My Name" is a paean to a girlfriend calling from the grave, and "Sister Ray" details one evening in the life of a group of sex workers. Morrison's account of the social setting in which *White Light / White Heat* was cut gives a sense of how a tainted love song like "The Gift" contrasts with those of the Velvet Underground's contemporaries: "The so-called 'Summer of Love' was a lovely summer in New York City. [...] Inspired by media hype and encouraged by deceitful songs on the radio ([Jefferson] Airplane, The Mama's & Papa's [*sic*]...) teenage ninnies flocked from Middle America out to the coast. [...] But behind them in Manhattan, all was suddenly quiet, clean, and beautiful. [...] And so at the height of the 'Summer of Love' we stayed in NYC and recorded *White Light / White Heat*."[7]

In this sense, while "The Gift"—and indeed the entirety of *White Light / White Heat*—appeared to be at odds with the general mood of 1967, the LP was prescient in terms of a cataclysmic change set to take place only months after its release in early 1968, as the utopic mood of the previous summer became dystopic with the assassinations of progressive political figures such as Martin Luther King, Jr., and Robert Kennedy. By early summer 1968, "The Gift" and *White Light / White Heat* were in unison with the energy of the times.

Using repetition to accentuate the macabre, "The Gift" recasts the very premise of what constitutes a love song. Rather than carefully crafting a melody using a verse / chorus structure, "The Gift" runs its narrative and instrumental components in parallel. Singularly non-emotive, it's one of the few tainted love songs to not be delivered in the first person.

1. Chris Roberts, *The Velvet Underground* (London: Palazzo Editions, 2022), 98.
2. Lou Reed, quoted in Lester Bangs, "Dead Lie the Velvets Underground R.I.P.: Long Live Lou Reed," *Creem* 3, no. 2 (May 1, 1971).
3. John Cale, quoted in Victor Bockris and Gerard Malanga, *Up Tight: The Velvet Underground Story* (New York: Cooper Square Press, 2003), 89.
4. The Velvet Underground, *White Light / White Heat*, Super Deluxe Edition, 2013.
5. At precisely this moment Reed adds a sound effect by stabbing a cantaloupe with a knife, as recommended by Frank Zappa, who was also working in New York's Mayfair Studios in September 1967. "He said, 'You'll get a better sound if you do it this way,'" Reed recalled. As quoted in the Velvet Underground, *White Light / White Heat*.
6. Sterling Morrison, quoted in Bockris and Malanga, *Up Tight*, 89.
7. Sterling Morrison, quoted in Roberts, *The Velvet Underground*, 99.

Antonio Carlos Jobim and Frank Sinatra,
"Off Key" (1969)

Inferiority

Antonio Carlos Jobim's "Off Key" uses the tainted
love song as a vehicle to respond to the widespread
belief about bossa nova—propagated when the style
first reached North America in the early '60s—that
its vocalists, particularly Astrud Gilberto and her
version of "The Girl from Ipanema," sing flat. The
song rotates on the inferiority complex its protagonist

has developed as a result of criticism of their supposedly off-key singing voice. Performed as a duet by Jobim and Frank Sinatra in 1969, the central tenet of "Off Key" becomes magnified because of the dynamic established between the most popular North American crooner with a South American songwriter and vocalist, transforming it into a tainted love song. So acute is the taint that "Off Key" remained unreleased in the composer's lifetime and was only made widely available in 2010.

The taint in "Off Key" is initially subtle, articulated in a version cut by João Gilberto in 1959, but becomes acute by the time of the duet with Sinatra in 1969. During the decade between the two versions, the song accrues a subtext based on how the creative exchange between Jobim and Sinatra—and more generally between Brazilian and North American musicians—is driven by the Cold War strategies of John F. Kennedy's administration in the early '60s. Without the State Department sponsoring Charlie Byrd's initial visit to Brazil in 1961—with Byrd and Stan Getz later being invited to perform at the White House—bossa nova likely wouldn't have reached its level of popularity in North America.

Capturing this cultural exchange, a CBS documentary on bossa nova from 1962 includes an interview with Jobim. Asked if he approves of bossa nova's success in North America, Jobim replies: "I do and I don't. There's a big commercial wave. This happened too in Rio. At the very beginning bossa nova was considered non-commercial music that nobody wanted to record. Then when bossa nova started to sell and everybody started to record bossa nova. [...] We had the same phenomena you have here now—bossa nova icebox, bossa nova washing machines, and bossa nova lawyers."[1]

"Off Key" reflects Jobim's ambivalence to bossa nova's reception outside of Brazil, accounting for its twisted nature. Jobim's collaboration with Sinatra, one of the many North American vocalists drawn to bossa nova, makes the twist more extreme. In the early '60s, Sinatra was linked with Kennedy's New Frontier more than any other popular musician, organizing the inaugural ball for the President-elect in 1961. Even when Kennedy distanced himself from the singer in 1962, Sinatra was still allied with the New Frontier, an association that continued more loosely throughout the Lyndon Johnson years (1964–68). Especially in the early '60s, Sinatra's baritone *is* the sound of the Cold War from the vantage point of those in power in North America.[2]

The twist in "Off Key" starts out relatively subtly. The original version of the song, sung by Gilberto, is in Portuguese and titled "Desafinado." The first attempt at translating the lyrics into English by John Hendricks was weak, as heard in a rendition by Ella Fitzgerald from 1962. It includes generic lines such as "A symphony conducted by the lighting of the moon / But our song of love is slightly out of tune"—in contrast to the later translation: "I wish I had an ear like yours, a voice that would behave / All I have is feelings and a voice God gave." By removing the song's taint, Hendricks's translation made it sound bland.

Providing something of a blueprint for the later version with Sinatra, Jobim's version from 1967, which uses Gene Lees's new translation—far more cutting than the one by Hendricks—elicits a poignant vocal performance from the composer. Jobim enters with the intro verse: "When I try to sing you say I'm off key / Why can't you see how much this hurts me?" The poignancy comes with the degree Jobim strains to sing the translated words to the melody. The result is dissonance.

Influenced by the teachings of the Brazil-based German classical composer Hans-Joachim Koellreutter, Jobim increasingly explores dissonance as the '60s unfold, easing his frequent arranger Claus Ogerman away from the temptations of Muzak (used on Jobim's first solo LP) toward more challenging orchestral charts. Beginning with the duet with Sinatra in 1969, and continuing with *Stone Flower* a year later, Jobim's work with the young Brazilian arranger Eumir Deodato emphasizes these moments of dissonance. Their version of "The Girl from Ipanema," released on the LP *Tide* (1970), reclaims this most iconic and melodic of Jobim's bossa nova songs by introducing sonic conflict into its arrangement. Initially, this new version of the song sounds like any other from the period, with the piano and flute picking out the melody against a soft rhythmic backdrop. But everything changes forty-nine seconds in, as the trombone and percussion abruptly break away from the moderate volume of the intro with a series of loud exaggerated thrusts, echoed a beat later by the string instruments. Nothing in bossa nova prepares you for this degree of instrumental contrast.

It is likely that Sinatra heard Jobim's LP *The Wonderful World of Antonio Carlos Jobim* (1965), which was arranged by the former's close collaborator Nelson Riddle; this may have cemented Sinatra's decision to work with Jobim. Whatever the deciding factor, by the end of 1966, Sinatra was planning an entire Jobim LP but with Ogerman arranging instead of Riddle. Jobim's sister recollects the excitement when "The phone rang at Veloso's bar one late afternoon. People called over to Tom [Jobim] and warned him it was a man speaking English. Tom answered, and on the other end was Frank Sinatra. He explained that somebody at Tom's house had given him that number. Sinatra invited Tom to record an album with him."[3]

The following month, Jobim flew to Los Angeles to start on the LP, with Ogerman bringing a freshly written arrangement to Jobim at the Beverly Hills Hotel each morning after working on it through the night. "Claus, do you think this is going to work?" Jobim asked in response to Ogerman's sparse charts.[4] "The pages looked so empty to [Jobim ... who] was used to having full scores," recalls Ogerman, "and my scores were really light."[5] But this was perfect for Sinatra. By not hampering the crooner with heavy arrangements, the sparseness grants Sinatra ample sonic space to move around in. In the meantime, rehearsals with Sinatra's pianist Bill Miller were underway, until the singer "knew every word and every nuance and every tone, every melody, perfectly," recalls Ogerman.[6] As one person attending the recording sessions noted, "it was like the World Softball Championships," with Sinatra, Jobim, and Ogerman carefully crafting the LP together.[7] Bossa nova may have been a foreign genre to the crooner but Sinatra took to it, as Nina Simone would a decade later with reggae. The key, it seems, is for the vocalist to sensitively register the passage of their métier through the new genre rather than attempting to restyle themselves after it.

A standout track on the first Jobim / Sinatra LP is "How Insensitive." The song is about a man's reflection on his lack of sensitivity when breaking off a romantic relationship. The lyrics read like they are providing the obverse side to "Off Key," as if written from the point of view of a North American male chastising themselves for being so insensitive when their Brazilian partner pledges their love by singing to them out of tune. That Jobim sings a verse in Portuguese—staying close to the melody and using some of the same vocal inflections as Sinatra—only adds to the precision of the overall call-and-response performance.

The success of Jobim and Sinatra's first LP led to a second spate of recordings in 1969. Jobim's sister recalls: "[Sinatra] wanted to know if Tom had any new music for an album. Tom replied that he 'only' had 140 new songs to be recorded. [...] Sinatra soon asked to see the scores and listen to the tapes, to be able to select and familiarize himself with the songs."[8] Where the first LP adds a sprinkling of classics from the American Songbook to the Jobim-heavy track list, the second collaboration features songs composed exclusively by Jobim. Jobim's vocals are also given more room, leading to the duet on "Off Key." This LP, arranged by Deodato, is more experimental. Each of the tracks feel heavier in tone. Partly this is due to Sinatra's voice, its viola-like timbre now assuming a cello-like depth.[9] But the arrangements also increase in weight, with Deodato eschewing the light orchestral touches of Ogerman in favor of more propulsive charts on the upbeat tracks and moments of dissonance on the ballads.

The duet version of "Off Key" opens with Sinatra singing the first lines of the introduction, "When I try to sing / You say I'm off key." Extremely rare for Sinatra, the phrase "off key" sounds flat. Compared to the first Jobim / Sinatra LP, the vocals are set very high in the mix, making for uncomfortable listening when they appear to go awry. Following Sinatra's lead, Jobim's reply—"Can't you see how much this hurts me?"—is also out of tune. Quickening the pace, as the main body of the song begins, a stronger rhythm kicks in. With it, the singing falls into tune, with Jobim taking the couplet "I wish I had an ear like yours / A voice that would behave." Toward the end of the song, Sinatra sings, "I took your picture with my trusty Rolleiflex," to which Jobim replies, "And now all I have developed is a complex." The translator, Lees, must have found their delivery of the "Rolleiflex / complex" rhyme humorous. The dissonance in Jobim and Sinatra's vocal performance in the intro may be painful, but it perfectly amplifies the inferiority complex the lyrics story. Latin America's involvement in the Cold War—including the 1962 Bay of Pigs invasion in Cuba and the US-sponsored coup d'état by the Brazilian military in 1964—would be enough to trigger an inferiority complex in any sensitive songwriter.

The dissonance evident in Deodato's arrangements caused Sinatra to make an unprecedented request: during live takes in the studio, Deodato was asked to play the notes from each phrase on a piano to provide a guide to the melody, fed through to Sinatra by way of an earpiece.[10] Evidently, the technique fails Sinatra on the first lines of the song, but thereafter it seems to work. "We've stopped the album," Sinatra explains in a radio interview at the time, "[as] there was some trepidation about releasing it."[11] Was the trepidation caused by the bum notes in the intro? Or was it due to the homoerotic undertones of two men singing about off-key love to one another? Whichever, what Sinatra refers to as "some trepidation" obviously grew to be substantial. The acuteness of the taint meant

"Off Key" was considered unfit for release both in 1969, when it was recorded, and in 1971, when much of the remaining Jobim / Sinatra session appeared on the LP *Sinatra and Company*. The song was not widely available until forty years later.

In addition to being a reflective comment on Latin American and US relations during the Cold War, "Off Key" also functions as a criticism of the contemporary shift toward dissidence in rock in North America (with the Doors and Jefferson Airplane, et al.) and their counterparts in Brazilian Tropicalia (with Tom Zé and Gal Costa). This parting shot, taken before the turn into the new decade, employs the tainted love song as a vehicle by introducing acute moments of dissonance, making "Off Key" a rare take on the genre.

1. Russ Bensley, dir., *The New Beat* (New York: CBS Broadcasting, 1962), https://www.jobim.org/jobim/handle/2010/4405.
2. For a broader discussion of the impact of the Cold War on the arts, see Serge Guilbault, *How New York Stole the Idea of Modern Art: Abstract Expressionism, Freedom, and the Cold War*, trans. Arthur Goldhammer (Chicago: University of Chicago Press, 1984).
3. Helena Jobim, *Antonio Carlos Jobim: An Illuminated Man* (Milwaukee, WI: Hal Leonard, 2011), Kindle.
4. Antonio Carlos Jobim, quoted in James Kaplan, *Sinatra: The Chairman* (New York: Anchor Books, 2016), 686.
5. Claus Ogerman, quoted in Kaplan, *Sinatra*, 686.
6. Ogerman, quoted in Kaplan, *Sinatra*, 687.
7. *Francis Albert Sinatra & Antonio Carlos Jobim*, Reprise, 1967, liner notes.
8. Jobim, *Antonio Carlos Jobim*.
9. On time and timbre in Sinatra's mature voice, see Richard Elliott, "September of My Years: Age and Experience in the Work of Frank Sinatra and Leonard Cohen," *The Late Voice: Time, Age and Experience in Popular Music* (London: Bloomsbury, 2015), 97–144.
10. *Francis Albert Sinatra & Antonio Carlos Jobim: The Complete Reprise Recordings*, the Concord Music Group, 2010, CD booklet.
11. Frank Sinatra, interview by Paul Compton, KGIL Radio, June 5, 1970, https://www.youtube.com/watch?v=BSj_Kp4meeo.

7

Soft Cell, "Tainted Love" (1981)

Tainted

Using sonic disruption and a synthesizer, in 1981
Soft Cell catapult "Tainted Love" out of the relatively
innocent context of Gloria Jones's soul-based original
from 1964. The public campness of glam in the early
'70s encouraged Soft Cell's vocalist Marc Almond to
come out in his teens, and later, to inject queerness
into the song—achieved by contrasting a hot vocal
with cool electronic backing culled from the late

'70s disco records of Donna Summer and Giorgio Moroder. The precise nature of the song's taint is accentuated by the way the band's visual styling plays on a bias still in place in the early '80s to equate gay love with tainted love.

When it came to recording "Tainted Love" in 1981, the second track on side one of the LP *Non-Stop Erotic Cabaret* (1981), the treatment "was stripped down, cold," says Almond, "with slinky electronics."[1] Producer Mike Thorne describes recording Almond's voice: "We went for a run-through of Marc's lead vocal before the sound was fully checked and settled. Experience shows it's always advisable to record the run-through. He let rip first time and that became the lead vocal on the final record without any adjustment."[2]

Almond's vocal performance bristles with emotion. The way Almond delivers the lines in the first verse—"Sometimes I feel I've got to run away / I've got to get away / From the pain you drive into the heart of me"—underscores the pleading message in the lyrics. In the chorus, the emotion gradually ramps up as Almond sings the lines "I give you all a boy could give you / Take my tears and that's not nearly all." The title phrase follows and is repeated, while a backing voice provides a distant echo. The later line "I toss and turn, I can't sleep at night" finds Almond pushing his voice to what feels like its furthest extreme, with the following refrain, "Don't touch me, please," infused with even more feeling. Lending the song an animated sense of emotion, the vocal is crucial to the taintedness of Soft Cell's version of "Tainted Love."

Soft Cell's Dave Ball first heard Jones's rendition of Ed Cobb's "Tainted Love" within the context of Northern soul. Emerging in Northern England and the Midlands in the late '60s and peaking by the mid-'70s, Northern soul nights were fueled by soul music featuring a heavy syncopated beat from North American cities like Chicago and Detroit.[3] On first hearing "Tainted Love," Ball was lured by the duality of what he passionately calls the song's "heartbreaking" yet "beautiful melodies."[4]

Parallel with Northern soul, Ball was also drawn to Kraftwerk and their genre-defining *Autobahn* (1974), captivated by what he calls the "haunting, otherworldly, slightly scary, yet pleasantly menacing quality" of the band's electrophilic sound.[5] To access it, Ball first acquired a miniKORG 800DV, and then a KORG Synthe-Bass SB-100. Ball's inventive use of technology was crucial to Soft Cell, evidenced by the snare-like noise mangled through a distinctive delay line to generate the opening "bink-bink" motif of "Tainted Love."

Frustrated with the nihilism driving punk, by 1977 Almond desired "songs about good times, songs to dance to, get drunk to, get high to."[6] Almond was particularly drawn to Donna Summer's 1977 hit "I Feel Love," and the way Summer and Giorgio Moroder set an electronic pulse rhythm to a machine beat with vocals that sounded both cold and sensual.[7] Vitally for Almond, the song "bridged the gap between Kraftwerk and David Bowie in the past [and the] nearer-to-home sounds of the Human League's 'Being Boiled' and *Reproduction*."[8] Summer and Moroder actually prototyped their distinctive sound two years before "I Feel Love" on "Love to Love You Baby." Written in response to the popularity of a mid-'70s rerelease of Serge Gainsbourg and Jane Birkin's 1969 tainted love song "Je t'aime moi non plus," Summer details the role sexuality played in their distinct version of disco:

"Giorgio [...] came in and said 'Je t'aime [moi non plus]' is on the market in London, it's selling again. And I said to him [...] why don't we make our own? [...] And he said, oh no, that's not your image. [...] And I said [...] why isn't it my image? [...] Out of that 'Love to Love You' evolved."[9]

Summer and Moroder's use of an electronic pulse rhythm set to a machine beat is crucial to how Soft Cell taint "Tainted Love." Written at the time Soft Cell were forming, Richard Dyer's 1979 essay "In Defense of Disco," published in the journal *Gay Left*, identifies the subversive potential of disco harnessed by the queer subculture of the late '70s.[10] This is largely based on the way disco rejects both the phallic machismo of rock and the emphasis on narrative lyrics in popular music. By restoring eroticism to the entire body, disco was key to the way Soft Cell aspired to press an electronic sound to more sensual ends.

The electronic effects underpinning "Tainted Love" amplify the sensuality desired: "At first it didn't occur to me," Almond writes (disingenuously?), "that my writhing about in leather and eyeliner gave the song a more subversive connotation."[11] By triggering this, the performative dimension to Almond's sexuality is crucial to the tainted nature of the track.[12] "The song took on a certain sleaziness," says Almond, "just because it was us doing it."[13]

Gloria Jones's comments on the song are apt in relation to Almond's: "I never liked the word 'tainted,' that was my problem. I just didn't understand [it] because I was a virgin [and] this was like 'Oh, I'm saying something nasty.'"[14] After first recording the song in 1964, Jones worked as a songwriter for Motown and occasionally released new music, relocating in the

62

early '70s to London to work as a vocal accompanist to her partner, Marc Bolan of T. Rex. With Bolan producing, Jones recorded a less frenetic version of "Tainted Love" for her solo LP *Vixen* (1976). With the proximity to Bolan's hedonistic lifestyle, Jones's feelings toward the song had obviously changed in the intervening years.

According to Almond, it was Bolan's corkscrewed hair and face covered in glitter that gave him license to perform his gay identity.[15] Like his glam contemporaries David Bowie and Roxy Music, a number of Bolan's songs were tainted love songs, from 1971's "Get It On" to 1974's "Venus Loon." Coincidentally, the LP with the latter song, *Zinc Alloy and the Hidden Riders of Tomorrow* (1974), was the first Bolan LP to feature Jones. Later, when Almond first hears the 1964 recording of "Tainted Love," he recalls Jones's name from its appearance on Bolan's LP. In Almond's mind, Jones's "Tainted Love" was already connected to Bolan's campness.

Soft Cell's "Tainted Love" remains alluring today partly because of the complexity of the way it fuses the duo's influences and synchronizes with the early '80s. Ball had Northern soul feeding into one ear and Kraftwerk in the other, while Almond had Moroder and Summer in one ear and Bolan in the other. Together, the diversity and mix of these sources ensured that for all its bareness, the track was dense with sonic signifiers, accruing further layers of meaning through the context in which it was released. That queerness was being more openly explored across fashion and film lent "Tainted Love" a unique potency. Still, Almond was frustrated at questions from prying journalists "all leading to the 'G' question—'Are you gay?'"[16] Courtesy of Almond

63

and Ball's intuitive strategy of sonic disruption, the taint was edgy enough to make it enticing, but not too dangerous to act as a barrier to widespread popularity, with "Tainted Love" reaching the much-coveted UK number one spot in September 1981.

1. Almond, *Tainted Life*, 111.
2. Mike Thorne, "Tainted Love," *Stereo Society*, March 1999, https://stereosociety.com/taintedlove/.
3. See David Nowell, *The Story of Northern Soul* (London: Portico, 1999).
4. Dave Ball, quoted in Guy Evans, dir., *Soft Cell: Say Hello, Wave Goodbye* (London: BBC, 2019).
5. Dave Ball, *Electronic Boy: My Life in and out of Soft Cell* (London: Omnibus Press, 2020), 54.
6. Almond, *Tainted Life*, 68.
7. See Dave Thompson, *I Feel Love: Donna Summer, Giorgio Moroder, and How They Reinvented Music* (Guilford, CT: Backbeat, 2021).
8. Almond, *Tainted Life*, 68. Not mentioned by Almond is the 1979 Moroder-produced track "Life in Tokyo" by Japan, which also broaches Bowie and disco.
9. Donna Summer, interview by Jim Esposito, *Rock's Backpages*, 1976, https://www.rocksbackpages.com/Library/Article/donna -summer-1976.
10. Richard Dyer, "In Defense of Disco" (1979), in *On Record: Rock, Pop and the Written Word*, ed. Simon Frith and Andrew Goodwin (London: Routledge, 1990), 351–58. For more alternative readings of disco, see Peter Shapiro, *Turn the Beat Around: The Secret History of Disco* (London: Faber and Faber, 2005).
11. Almond, *Tainted Life*, 117–18.
12. See Philip Brett, Elizabeth Wood, and Gary C. Thomas, eds. *Queering the Pitch: The New Gay and Lesbian Musicology* (London: Routledge, 1994).
13. Almond, *Tainted Life*, 111.
14. *Tainted Love: The Story behind the Song* (Amsterdam: Top 2000 à Go-Go, 2010), https://www.youtube.com/watch?v=ViWAVwY7LtU&ab _channel=Top2000agogo.
15. Almond, *Tainted Life*, 22.
16. Almond, *Tainted Life*, 107.

8

Paul McCartney, "Here Today" (1982)

Grief

Written six months after John Lennon's murder in
December 1980, "Here Today" is an articulation of
Paul McCartney's grief, a "love song to John"—a
tainted love song.[1] The song uses quietness as its sonic
key, with McCartney pressing the soft pedal even
more than usual. As a result, the song is concentrated
within a very limited range; even slight increases
in volume and emphasis are noticeable.

With "Here Today" McCartney proves himself to be as complex a songwriter as his onetime partner. Lennon's own attempts at the tainted love song started with his 1965 "Girl," addressing the warped dynamic of an amorous relationship ("pain would lead to pleasure"), and continued with the 1968 heart-wrenching love song directed toward his late mother, "Julia." By contrast, McCartney never ventured into tainted love territory in the '60s, tending toward romantic ballads typified by 1964's "And I Love Her." With the exception of 1966's "For No One," written in the third person as a way to distance himself from the loveless marriage being described, when McCartney does explore a more strained dynamic in a romantic relationship, it's usually with a view to resolving it, as per "We Can Work It Out." In the same way that McCartney seldom probes into tensions in romantic relationships, the "Mother Mary" figure appearing in the opening lines of his 1969 "Let It Be" is not elaborated on, despite referring to his own mother who, like Lennon's, died during his teens. Throughout the decade when they were working together, only Lennon explored a more complex range of emotions; McCartney steered clear of complexity and taint.

The 1971 song "Dear Friend," which marks the demise of their friendship, is McCartney's first attempt at a tainted love song. Like "Here Today," the song is premised on a dialogue with Lennon. Written in the form of a letter, "Dear Friend" starts with "Dear friend, what's the time? / Is this really the borderline?" The two songwriters, once so close, had reached an impasse following the split of their band in 1970 and their respective snipes at one another. Lennon's animosity was triggered by the lyrics of McCartney's 1971 "Too Many People," which criticizes

66

Lennon and Yoko Ono's Bed-Ins for Peace. A few months later, Lennon replies with the vituperative "How Do You Sleep," referring to two of McCartney's songs with the stinging couplet "The only thing you done was yesterday / And since that's gone, you're just another day." A few months later again, and on the opening lines of the second verse of "Dear Friend," McCartney sings, "Dear friend, throw the wine / I'm in love with a friend of mine." McCartney's declaration of platonic love at precisely the moment when their friendship was at its lowest ebb following their band's demise is striking. But "Dear Friend" does not feel fully resolved sonically. An instrumental section follows the opening two verses, after which they are simply repeated. Demos released in 2018 reveal McCartney seemingly struggling to develop "Dear Friend" any further than the second verse, filling in the rest of the song by humming the melody—replaced by an orchestral treatment on the LP version. The demos give insight into how McCartney was unwilling, or perhaps unable, to further flesh out the initial idea for "Dear Friend" even on the final version on the LP, a tendency toward the fragmentary that is typical of tracks of the early '70s from *McCartney* (1970) through to *Ram* (1971) and *Wild Life* (1971).

The next time McCartney addresses Lennon in song is a decade later with "Here Today," written in the summer of 1981, less than six months after Lennon's murder. McCartney describes "just sitting quietly in this little room with my guitar and these chords starting coming out and I started [having] these thoughts as if I was talking to myself to John about our relationship and stuff."[2] This time McCartney grapples with the difficult aspects of their relationship head on, taking the song to a point of conclusion both structurally and lyrically. As a result, the song packs a real punch. Like "Dear Friend," "Here Today" is also inspired by a traumatic event, this time one with a tragic finality. In McCartney's hands, the danger would be for such a tribute to be overly sentimental. That "Here Today" is premised on the tension between the songwriting partners staged in the form of an intimate conversation rescues it from this fate. McCartney describes his approach: "What had been going through my head was this idea that if you [John] were here today what would you [...] say about [...] me writing a song about you?"[3]

The status of "Here Today" as a tainted love song is compounded through McCartney's declaration of platonic love for Lennon and his elaboration of their differences. Set in a minor key, and using a gentle, almost whispered voice accompanied by arpeggio-style acoustic guitar, the song's opening lines are: "And if I say / I really knew you well / What would your answer be?" In an interview, McCartney describes imagining Lennon's response coming in the form of a cloud parting in the sky and Lennon blowing a raspberry at him.[4] Appropriately, Lennon's perceived reply is voiced by McCartney in the song using an exaggerated blue note—the nearest in musical harmony to a raspberry—struck with the word "you" in the first line of the second verse: "Well, knowing you / You'd probably laugh / And say that we were worlds apart." Introducing a different vocal texture into the song, the "ooh" of the chorus is sung as if to remind the listener, lest anyone forget, of the musicians' shared origins.

With the first line of the middle section, "But as for me / I still remember how it was before," McCartney refutes Lennon's presumed response to the song.

"I'm sort of saying," McCartney commented later, "even though you blow that raspberry I really did know you."[5] To emphasize the line, both the guitar and the voice become more strident, rising slightly in volume; the quietness is momentarily broken. To lend ballast to McCartney's claim, the following verses provide a portal into two key moments from their shared past. The couplet "What about the time we met / Well, I suppose that you could say that we were playing hard to get" refers to the fabled meeting between the two in 1957 when McCartney auditioned for Lennon at a garden fete in Woolton, Liverpool. Evidently, they were slightly cool toward one another, with McCartney being impressed by Lennon's lyrical style but not so much his coarse nature, and Lennon recognizing McCartney's talent but deliberating over whether he should replace a current member of his band. The second key moment from their shared past, referred to with the line "What about the night we cried," recalls McCartney and Lennon being waylaid by a hurricane in a hotel in Key West, Florida, during a US tour in 1964. In an interview, McCartney remembers the two drinking and discussing a wide range of subjects. "It was the only time we'd cried together," McCartney later said, "one of those drunken crying sessions."[6] Deploying a device from film, the first lines of these lyrics are treated with exaggerated echo as if to emphasize that they're memories. A final verse, including the line "If I say I really loved you / What would your answer be," a last chorus, and "Here Today" ends. At two minutes and twenty-seven seconds, the track is short, but as the final song on side one of *Tug of War*, it leaves a distinct impression on the listener, seeming to cloud the air in any given room.

Critics often say that after 1970, McCartney perpetually fails to scale the heights reached in the '60s while collaborating with Lennon. But what if the opposite is actually the case? What if the tainted love song allows McCartney's writing to improve in quality, as prototyped with "Dear Friend," and reaching a peak with "Here Today"? A song as emotionally complex and thoroughly resolved as "Here Today" would never have been attempted by McCartney in the '60s—such nuance would have been Lennon's domain. The appalling events of December 1980 seem to free McCartney from having to define himself in contrast to Lennon's sensibility. The result is "Here Today," wherein McCartney's oft-criticized lyrical sensibility finally reaches the same level as his widely acknowledged melodic one.

"Here Today" represents a stage in McCartney's grieving process. As per the pattern of grieving, McCartney's initial response to Lennon's murder was denial, surely visible when he was forced by a journalist to make a statement on the day of the murder. Exiting George Martin's Air Studios in London, McCartney is asked, "How did you find out about [Lennon's murder]?" "I got a phone call this morning," McCartney replies. "From whom?" the reporter probes. "Er, from a friend of mine," McCartney responds, wavering. The questions keep coming: "What were you recording today?" "I was just listening to some stuff as I just didn't want to sit at home," he replies. A further inane question: "Why?" "Because I didn't feel like it," McCartney says, sounding annoyed. "What time did you hear the news?" "This morning some time." "Very early?" the reporter presses. "Yeah, drag isn't it," McCartney says before ducking into a waiting car.[7] Over the following weeks, the "drag, isn't it?" comment would come to haunt him as denial gives way to anger, directed at Mark Chapman, Lennon's murderer, with McCartney calling him "the jerk of all jerks."[8] The penultimate stage in McCartney's public grieving is bargaining, finding him attempting to think through his dynamic with Lennon and how things could have been different. Composed six months after Lennon's death, there's a sense that "Here Today" comes from this moment of grieving, partly accounting for why the song is premised on such an unusual sentiment: McCartney's projection of Lennon's perception of their relationship.

In February 1981, a few months prior to McCartney composing "Here Today," and less than two months after Lennon's death, an unusual thing happened. During the recording sessions for the song "Get It" from *Tug of War*, Carl Perkins—whose compositions Lennon and McCartney frequently covered in the early '60s—plays Paul and Linda McCartney his newly written song "My Old Friend," with its chorus including the refrain "My old friend / Won't you think about me / Every now and then." The McCartneys' response surprises Perkins: "After I finished Paul was crying, tears were rolling down his cheeks, and Linda said, 'Carl, thank you so much […] he's crying, and he needed to. He hasn't been able to really break down since that happened to John.' She said that the last words that John said to Paul in the hallway of the Dakota building were […] 'Think about me every now and then, old friend.'"[9]

That Perkins composes a song using the same words Lennon had said to McCartney during their last meeting is nothing less than an incredible coincidence. As it was, the coincidence was fortuitous because the nature of Perkins's country-tinged "My Old Friend" seems to absolve McCartney of the need to revert to his default mode and write an overly sentimental ballad of his own. Instead, emphasizing quietness, McCartney writes "Here Today." In this sense, the tainted love song allows McCartney to find his voice at a crucial juncture as a songwriter, particularly as a lyricist. The price of losing Lennon may be one McCartney would have preferred not to have paid, but his death accommodated his strongest solo work to date.

1. Paul McCartney, *The Lyrics: 1956 to the Present* (London: Allen Lane, 2021), 277.
2. Paul McCartney, *Tug of War*, 1982, promo cassette, https://www.youtube.com/watch?v=AJ-SkJrioAA.
3. McCartney, *Tug of War*.
4. Tom Doyle, *Man on the Run: Paul McCartney in the 1970s* (Edinburgh: Polygon, 2014), 290.
5. Doyle, *Man on the Run*, 290.
6. Paul McCartney, *Tug of War*, Super Deluxe Edition, 2015, 87.
7. Paul McCartney, interview, ABC News, December 9, 1980, https://www.youtube.com/watch?v=L19kVCuzjYo.
8. Paul McCartney, interview by Jonathan Ross, *The Jonathan Ross Show*, ITV, December 6, 2014.
9. Carl Perkins, "My Old Friend Backstory—Carl Perkins with Paul McCartney," 1996, https://youtu.be/rn19iLYFZKw.

Charlotte and Serge Gainsbourg,
"Lemon Incest" (1984)

Provocation

In 2019, at the height of #MeToo, replying to
an interviewer, Charlotte Gainsbourg responds
to long-held assumptions about the tainted dynamic
portrayed in the 1984 duet she recorded with her
father at the age of thirteen. "It was about the love
of a father to his daughter and the other way around,"
Charlotte Gainsbourg says, "[and] it was very explicit

in the song that he was saying 'the love that we will *never* make together.'"[1] Using a strategy of sonic contrast to realize what Serge Gainsbourg referred to as a "provocation," "Lemon Incest" plays on perceptions of one of society's most taboo subjects. "I am a man subject to vertigo and I think that incest is—vertigo," Serge Gainsbourg commented, "[and] I imagine that it could be superb, but at the same time an atrocity."[2] Because of its subject, "Lemon Incest" triggered a controversy that continues to cling to the song.

Leading up to the composition of "Lemon Incest," Serge Gainsbourg began developing an alter ego: Gainsbarre. The lyrics to the 1981 "Ecce Homo" detail "Gainsbarre's signature style / Features blue jeans, three-night / Stubble, cigars / And bouts of depression." The Gainsbarre era had been preceded by a period of intense creativity for Serge Gainsbourg. From the early '70s into the '80s, Serge Gainsbourg composed countless inventive melodies on a sequence of LPs starting with *Histoire de Melody Nelson* (1971) and running through *Vu de l'extérieur* (1973), *Rock Around the Bunker* (1975), *L'homme à tête de chou* (1976), and *Aux armes et cætera* (1979). These melodies are often partnered with provocative lyrics exploring a range of subjects from sexuality and pornography to French nationalism and Nazism. Fueled by alcoholism, from 1981 until his death a decade later, Gainsbourg turned away from the sophisticated orchestral sensibility he developed throughout the '70s to the banal instrumentation of Euro-pop as a tray on which to serve Gainsbarre's lyrics of a more perverse, if not perverted, nature. As the desire to provoke increased, the musicality of the tracks dropped off.

To prepare for the contrasting duet he was seeking, Serge Gainsbourg recommended that his daughter listen to two songs in preparation: "He told me that exact song ['Lay, Lady, Lay'], saying it was one of the greats," explains Charlotte Gainsbourg, "[and] 'Somewhere Over the Rainbow' sung by a young Judy Garland."[3] The apparent lewdness of the lyrics of Bob Dylan's 1969 song delivered with his country baritone (the song was originally written for *Midnight Cowboy* [1969]) and the genuine sweetness of Garland's soprano on *The Wizard of Oz* (1939) soundtrack are deftly pitted against one another on "Lemon Incest." With Serge Gainsbourg taking on the male role while his daughter assumes the female one, the polarizing of gender roles in "Lemon Incest" contrasts sharply with explorations by a younger generation of musicians at the time, typified by Prince, who turns to the theme of incest on "Sister" from 1980 by using falsetto for the male character and casting the female character as the elder of the two.

Using a shrill, wine glass–shattering soprano, Charlotte Gainsbourg sings the opening lines to "Lemon Incest" in French: "The love we'll never make together / Is the most beautiful, the most violent / The purest, the headiest." "I understood the pleasure he got from [...] hearing me hit those high notes," remembers Charlotte Gainsbourg, "and my voice breaking a bit. And those were things he was aiming at."[4] To his daughter's lines in the song, Serge Gainsbourg replies: "Exquisite silhouette, luscious child / My flesh and blood / Oh! My baby, my soul." The next verse repeats the format of the first, with just a subtle change in lyric. Charlotte Gainsbourg sings, "The love we'll never make together / Is the most uncommon, the most troubling / The purest, the rawest." To which Serge Gainsbourg drawls the reply, "Exquisite silhouette, luscious child / My flesh and blood / Oh! My baby, my soul." The extreme dissimilarity in vocal delivery and timbre continues throughout the track. Contrast is the sonic key as it increases the lyrics' ability to provoke by amplifying their disturbing nature.

Instrumentally, Serge Gainsbourg moves away from both the crack UK rhythm section he contracted for much of the late '60s and early '70s, and the duo of Sly Dunbar and Robbie Shakespeare he worked with between 1979 and 1981, toward a more generic synth-based pop in the mid-'80s. In search of this sound, he first approaches Nile Rodgers after hearing the LP the latter coproduced with Billy Rush, *Trash It Up!* (1983) by Southside Johnny and the Asbury Jukes. After Rodgers turned the project down in favor of working with Madonna on *Like a Virgin* (1984), Serge Gainsbourg opted to work with just Rush. "We didn't speak," Rush says of their first day in New York's Power Station Studio, "I sensed he was unsure and measuring me up. [...] I chose a rhythm, stuck on a bass, threw in some keyboards and guitars."[5] Serge Gainsbourg took the tape away and returned the next day keen to continue. As the producer, Rush chose the musicians, including Steve and George Sims, from David Bowie's "Serious Moonlight" tour (1983). While the overall sound lacks the artfulness of *Histoire de Melody Nelson*, or the funk-fueled pop of Bowie's Rodgers-produced *Let's Dance* (1983) from a year before, the gaudy synth-based sound drives home the twisted nature of the lyrics. The chintzy instrumentation is a sonic equivalent to the cheap pun underpinning the song. In French, its title translates to "inceste de citron," which sounds very

much like "un zeste de citron" — "a zest of lemon."
By using the pun, Serge Gainsbourg makes it clear
that while the song may express a desire for incest,
it does not suggest that actual incest has occurred.

"Lemon Incest" builds on duets, from the late
'60s onward, with Charlotte Gainsbourg's mother,
Jane Birkin. While the older man / younger woman
dynamic is explicitly played out on the couple's
1969 single "Je t'aime moi non plus," it implicitly
structures the lyrical themes of the LP *Histoire de
Melody Nelson*, cut two years later. On the third
verse of the song "Ballade de Melody Nelson,"
Serge Gainsbourg says, "She had a wild streak that..."
in spoken-word French, only to be interrupted
by Birkin completing it by whispering the name
"Melody Nelson" into the mic. In the next line,
Serge Gainsbourg describes Melody Nelson as "Such
an adorable little tomboy / And such a delicious child."
The contrast between Serge Gainsbourg's baritone
and Birkin's whispered soprano lends the track an
intriguing texture, doubling the narrative spun by the
lyrics. Lacking the delicate arrangement of "Ballade
de Melody Nelson" — especially the delicious run of
bass notes at the end of each verse — "Lemon Incest"
amplifies the implicit dynamic staged by the earlier
duet with Birkin to almost grotesque proportions.
With Birkin breaking off their relationship in 1981,
after being repelled by the excesses of the Gainsbarre
character, Serge Gainsbourg's attentions shifted to
writing songs for both his eldest daughter, Charlotte,
and his new partner, Bambou.

The Lolita archetype derived from Vladimir
Nabokov's 1955 novel is key to "Lemon Incest."
Claiming that "*Lolita* hit me right in the face,"[6]
Serge Gainsbourg attempted to set Nabokov's words

to music for a projected song on *Serge Gainsbourg N° 4* (1962). But with director Stanley Kubrick's film soon to be released, the request was denied. Beginning with a tune written for France Gall in 1966, "Les Sucettes," progressing with "Je t'aime moi non plus" in 1968 and "Ballade de Melody Nelson" in 1972, and culminating with "Lemon Incest" in 1984, Serge Gainsbourg was forced to develop his own lyrical response to the Lolita theme instead.

In her essay "Brigitte Bardot and the Lolita Syndrome," published in the August 1959 issue of *Esquire*, Simone de Beauvoir focuses on the attraction of the Lolita archetype for men of Serge Gainsbourg's generation, tracing how the role of Lolita is actualized by Bardot in the film *And God Created Woman* (1956).[7] Beginning with the original version of "Je t'aime moi non plus," Serge Gainsbourg's songs written for Bardot play through this logic. But by the late '60s, Bardot sings in a much lower register, the contrast between her voice and Serge Gainsbourg's not being as effective as Birkin's is a year later or his daughter's will be in 1984.

Following "Lemon Incest," Charlotte Gainsbourg records her debut LP, *Charlotte for Ever* (1986), which includes the song "Oh Daddy Oh," and then turns to film, appearing in *Kung Fu Master* (1988) and *The Sun Also Shines at Night* (1990). Directed by Birkin's brother, *The Cement Garden* (1993), an adaption of Ian McEwan's 1978 novel detailing an incestuous relationship between a brother and sister, is one of Charlotte Gainsbourg's first lead roles. Later, her star role in Lars von Trier's *Nymphomaniac* in 2013 ensures that controversy centered on illegal sexual relationships remained a constant in her life. Charlotte Gainsbourg only returns to music in 2006 with the LP *5:55*, conceived partly in collaboration with the French electronic duo Air. This was followed by a regular stream of LPs, including *IRM* (2009) and *Stage Whisper* (2011), both produced by Beck, and *Rest* (2017), produced by SebastiAn. On "Lying with You" Gainsbourg imagines her nineteen-year-old self, lying next to her father as he dies in 1991. The song finds Charlotte Gainsbourg recounting their shared history in song. One verse refers to their experience making "Lemon Incest" by recalling the way her father used her as a puppet in the song: "So let me imagine / That I was alone to love you / With a pure love of a darling girl / Poor chilled puppet." Written by someone looking back at their younger self, first to 1991 and her father's death, and then further back to their duet on "Lemon Incest" in 1984, the lyrics give a sense of Charlotte Gainsbourg coming to terms with the complexity of their relationship.

The set list for one of Charlotte Gainsbourg's recent tours includes the radically revised version of "Lemon Incest," with her taking on both vocal roles. In early 2020, at the Théâtre Antique d'Arles, Gainsbourg sits at a keyboard and makes her way through "Lemon Incest," altering the pitch of her voice to develop a more subtle sense of contrast compared to the 1984 version. With her father having been dead for almost three decades at this point, Charlotte Gainsbourg comfortably addresses the family legacy. The listener is left with the sense that the ultimate transgression her father committed was to have played the role of ventriloquist to explore ideas around incest. The live version of "Lemon Incest" suggests that Gainsbourg has now fully accepted this and is able to revisit the duet productively. Boosting her agency by assuming both vocal roles, and thereby reducing the level of sonic contrast, Gainsbourg performs a balancing act to ensure the tainted love song most associated with her remains relevant, in a very different age, while maintaining its provocative nature.

1. Charlotte Gainsbourg, "Amplified: Charlotte Gainsbourg," interview by Dan Harris, ABC News, February 9, 2010, https://youtu.be/OlH1pxG_SxA.
2. Serge Gainsbourg, quoted in Sylvie Simmons, *Serge Gainsbourg: A Fistful of Gitanes* (Boston: Da Capo Press, 2002), 110.
3. Charlotte Gainsbourg, "Charlotte Gainsbourg on the Music of Her Life," Red Bull Music Academy, Paris, 2017, https://youtu.be/2RCrJGGu3go.
4. Gainsbourg, "Charlotte Gainsbourg on the Music of Her Life."
5. Billy Rush, quoted in Simmons, *Serge Gainsbourg*, 108.
6. Jeremy Allen, *Relax Baby Be Cool: The Artistry and Audacity of Serge Gainsbourg* (London: Jawbone Books, 2021), 153.
7. Simone de Beauvoir, "Brigitte Bardot and the Lolita Syndrome," trans. Bernard Frechtman, *Esquire*, August 1, 1959, https://classic.esquire.com/article/1959/8/1/brigitte-bardot-and-the-lolita-syndrome.

10

PJ Harvey and Nick Cave, "Henry Lee" (1996)

Murder

While PJ Harvey and Nick Cave have composed
many love songs, the tainted love song occupies a
special place in their respective oeuvres. Cave's LP
Murder Ballads (1996) is exclusively devoted to the
form, a genre based on stories of gruesome crimes
of passion (though not always love songs). Typically,
murder ballad lyrics mix tender observations about
a character's, say, lily-white hands, with appalling

scenes of bloodshed. If murder is the theme of "Henry Lee," then vocal harmony is the sonic key through which it's parleyed. Despite the role harmony plays in the performance, "Henry Lee" is also one of the few murder ballads that lyrically flips the script, with the woman murdering the man.

Cave initially offered Harvey two songs to choose from to perform solo on his album. Harvey opted for "Henry Lee," insisting on it being a duet. Positioned as the second track on side one, the song opens at a funereal pace, with the piano marking out a circular motif as Harvey's deep, full voice commands, "Get down, get down, little Henry Lee / And stay all night with me," declaring, "You won't find a girl in this damn world / That will compare with me." Against a swell in the instrumentation, with the piano working higher up the scale, the "La-la-la-la-Lee" refrain in the chorus is sung together, with Cave shadowing Harvey by singing just beneath her. "I can't get down / And I won't get down / And stay all night with thee," Cave replies, "For the girl I have in that merry green land / I love far better than thee." A second chorus follows, and then Cave takes the next action-packed verse: "And with a little pen-knife held in her hand / She plugged him through and through." The remaining verses tell how the woman throws Lee down a well. With Cave continuing to hold the melody, the final chorus finds Harvey's voice soaring higher, the only concession to the traditional role historically assumed by a female singer in a duet.

Focusing on carnal desire and emotional carnage, Harvey has a history of composing tainted love songs. On the LP *Dry* (1993), released three years before *Murder Ballads*, Harvey explores the macabre with lines such as "Rest your head on me / I'll smooth it nicely / Rub it better 'til it bleeds." In "Down by the Water," from *To Bring You My Love* (1995), recorded just prior to "Henry Lee," Harvey draws on the same macabre theme as Cave later does on "Where the Wild Roses Grow," another duet on *Murder Ballads*. "I had to lose her / To do her harm," rasps Harvey on "Down by the Water," "I heard her holler / I heard her moan." No wonder Harvey slips into character so smoothly as the murderer of Henry Lee.

Cave's output is similarly littered with macabre tainted love songs touching on murder. "I've always enjoyed writing narrative songs," says Cave, "and I've always especially enjoyed writing about murder."[1] "Little Girl Tree," from *The Firstborn Is Dead* (1985), includes the lines "Oh, little girl the truth would be / An axe in thee," while "Jack the Ripper," from *Henry's Dream* (1992), describes the way "She strikes me down with a fist of lead / We bed in a bucket of butcher's knives." Summing up Cave's fascination with murder, the song "Loverman," on the LP prior to *Murder Ballads*, *Let Love In* (1994), bluntly exclaims, "M is for murder me." By no surprise, Cave had been considering devoting an entire LP to the form for over a decade prior to the release of *Murder Ballads* in 1996.[2]

"Henry Lee" would not have been possible without Cave's fascination with Leonard Cohen. Cave included a version of Cohen's "Avalanche" from *Songs of Love and Hate* (1971) on the first Nick Cave and the Bad Seeds LP, *From Her to Eternity* (1984). For Cave, Cohen's *Songs of Love and Hate* "remains one of the seminal albums that completely changed the kind of music I would make. [...] It was really the first record that showed a way where it was possible to take some of the kind of dark, self-lacerating visions we found in much of the European poetry and literature [...] and apply them to a kind of rock sound."[3] While Cohen never writes a murder ballad, some songs—including 1968's "The Butcher," detailing the story of a lamb being slaughtered, and "Dress Rehearsal Rag," from *Songs of Love and Hate*, centering on a man considering slitting his throat when shaving—express a penchant for the macabre.

Just prior to "Henry Lee," Harvey recorded *To Bring You My Love*, an LP focusing heavily on her vocals. "I'm very interested in the voice," Harvey says, "and its capacity to change words."[4] "The sounds I like aren't 'pure,'" Harvey continues, "[they] actually come from harming my voice by smoking and drinking too much, so it sounds gravelly."[5] The result is a series of richly textured vocal performances, a tendency that the duet with Cave plays through.

In "Henry Lee" Harvey veers close to aspects of the vocal character of Nina Simone, a singer he frequently channels. "Even [Simone's] most beautiful love songs," writes Cave, evidence an "exhilarating collision of opposing forces—love and scorn."[6] On the occasions when Simone performs a ballad emphasizing this scorn, as per her interpretation of Billie Holiday's "Strange Fruit," the effect is devastating. Channeling Simone, Harvey's voice dovetails neatly with Cave's baritone. A year after recording the song, Cave commented on how, like Harvey, he too was beginning to exert "more control than I used to," having "accepted the fact that my voice will always sound the same way: morose, melancholy, lugubrious, plaintive," rather than just plain gnarly as on earlier records.[7] All of these influences and their respective tonal qualities are brought to bear on Harvey and Cave's vocal performances on "Henry Lee," leading to a rich harmonic texture full of subtle inflections.

Of all the songwriters in *Tainted Love: From Nina Simone to Kendrick Lamar*, Cave is the only one to identify with and draw so heavily on the genre, and to dive into it historically. The origins of "Henry Lee" stretch back to the eighteenth century, with thenarrative presenting the story of a protagonist who informs a jealous woman his heart belongs to a more beautiful woman elsewhere. On hearing this, the woman lures him with a kiss before stabbing him to death. The earliest known recording of the song is by the blues singer Dick Justice in 1929; folksinger Judy Henske included a rendition of the song on her debut LP released in 1962. Cave's version uses elements from each of these variants, molding them into an effective vehicle for a duet.

The music video shoot for "Henry Lee" was one of the first times Harvey and Cave met.[8] Dressed alike and sporting the same long, goth-black hair replete with pale white complexions, the chemistry between them is palpable. Vamping for the camera, when Cave mimes the line about how the woman "plugged him through and through," Harvey affectionately caresses his face. And during the chorus, when they sing in harmony, they are holding one another's hands. "We didn't know each other well," says Cave, "and this thing happens while we're making the video. There's a certain awkwardness, and afterwards it's like, oh…"[9] Following the video shoot, an intense romantic relationship ensued. On his *Red Hand Files* blog, Cave reveals feeling good at the time, "with a talented and beautiful young singer for a girlfriend," until the phone rang. "I pick up the phone and it's Polly. 'Hi,' I say. 'I want to break up with you.' 'Why?!'

I ask. 'It's just over,' she says."[10] Twenty-five years later, Cave is evidently still upset by it. This episode lends "Henry Lee" an unintended taint.

Cave's response in song comes directly after the breakup, with "Where Do We Go Now but Nowhere?" and "Far from Me" from *The Boatman's Call* (1997). Harvey's rejoinder, of sorts, comes two years later, on the LP *Is This Desire?* (1998). These new songs find Cave and Harvey singing in the first person. Perhaps more than its composition, the experience of both recording the song "Henry Lee" and shooting the video—and the relationship it ignited—forced Harvey and Cave to address aspects of their respective approaches to songwriting. "Henry Lee" was to be the last of a type for Harvey and Cave, as the vocal harmony used as a counterpoint to its gruesome lyrics was played out in real life, impacting both songwriters acutely.

1. Nick Cave, quoted in Santi Elijah Holley, *Murder Ballads* (London: Bloomsbury, 2021), 2.

2. See Nick Cave, interview by Nanni Jacobson, Los Angeles, 1997, https://www.youtube.com/watch?v=Uf-NwfDznLM&ab_channel=Nanni_J.

3. Nick Cave, quoted in Sylvie Simmons, *I'm Your Man: The Life of Leonard Cohen* (London: Vintage, 2013), 361.

4. PJ Harvey, quoted in David Cavanagh, "Nemesis in a Scarlet Dress," *Independent*, February 25, 1995, https://www.independent.co.uk/arts-entertainment/nemesis-in-a-scarlet-dress-1574777.html.

5. PJ Harvey, quoted in Simon Reynolds, "PJ Harvey: What Makes Polly Scream?," *i-D*, November 1993.

6. Nick Cave, *Red Hand Files* 104, July 2020, https://www.theredhandfiles.com/protest-song-that-you-greatly-admire/.

7. Nick Cave, quoted in Mat Snow, *Nick Cave: Sinner Saint: The True Confessions* (London: Plexus, 2011), 174.

8. For a detailed analysis of Harvey's video performances, see Abigail Gardner, *PJ Harvey and Music Video Performance* (London: Routledge, 2020).

9. Cave, quoted in Snow, *Nick Cave*, 190.

10. Nick Cave, *Red Hand Files* 57, August 2019, https://www.theredhandfiles.com/your-relationship-with-pj-harvey/.

II

Little Simz, "I Love You, I Hate You" (2021)

Conflicted

Little Simz's portrayal of a single mother in the TV drama *Top Boy* connects with her 2021 song "I Love You, I Hate You," which focuses on the rapper's conflicted feelings about her absent father. The taint is courtesy of Simz's reflection on her father's leaving the family home when she was young, articulated using a series of contrasts—lyrically, instrumentally, and vocally.

The last track on side one of *Sometimes I Might Be Introvert* (2021), "I Love You, I Hate You" identifies a persistent emotional trigger for Simz. "As much as it's written about him, it's not about him," says Simz, as "[the song's] about me and my feelings about it all and how this is affecting my relationships."[1] Turning the title "I Love You, I Hate You" into a hook that's repeated throughout the song effectively conveys the sense of someone perpetually changing their mind from one extreme to the other. "I think I understood that this [issue] is bigger than me," Simz says, "and I know this [song] has the potential to help someone."[2] "I Love You, I Hate You" gives voice to anyone harboring conflicted feelings about an absent parent.

In the second verse, Simz raps: "Or what kind of external family shit up on your plate / But I understand wanting, needing an escape." Asked about these lyrics, Simz responds: "that's about thinking I'm understanding, 'You could have had your own childhood traumas'. [...] We grew up very different. You look at my life and think, 'You are very privileged,' [while] you grew up in Nigeria. So, it was trying to approach it from a place of emotional empathy."[3] Despite this empathy, Simz describes still feeling hurt and not shying away from the fact. The way the lyrics oscillate between emotional empathy and stinging criticism winds Simz's conflicted emotions into a tightly bound coil.

"A song like 'I Love You, I Hate You' couldn't have been on my first album," explains Simz, as "I don't think I was emotionally mature enough to tackle something like that."[4] Instead, Simz's first LP, *A Curious Tale of Trials + Persons* (2015), turns to issues ranging from the role of women in rap to the tension a performer feels as they move between their private and public selves. Simz's sophomore LP, *Stillness in Wonderland* (2016), uses the trope of the fairy tale to explore subjects as various as new romance, toxic relationships, and emotional vulnerability. "Sherbet Sunset," the final track on Simz's next LP, *GREY Area* (2019), deals with the complex issue of what happens when love turns into hate. After Simz professes to have overcome the disappointment of a failed relationship, the last line of the song flips the situation completely. "Chill, I'm good, I got it / I never lost it," spits Simz, "Or am I just lying to myself to skip the topic?" Here Simz admits to being conflicted when it comes to making a decision about whether to even face difficult emotional issues. Two years later, when the producer Inflo presented a viable backing track for "I Love You, I Hate You," Simz's response was "that beat's shit!"—rejecting it as a way to avoid the song's subject.[5] Eventually, instead of skipping her conflicted feelings, Simz persevered and embraced them.

Simz's confrontational tone on "I Love You, Hate You" finds a rare resonance with Speech Debelle's 2009 "Daddy's Little Girl." The song's opening line confronts the same love/hate dynamic that Simz's hinges on over a decade later: "Daddy I think I love you 'cause I hate you so much that I must love you." In the same verse, Debelle describes the way her father "Hurt me, scarred me so deeply I have trouble / Committing to any man 'cause I think he's / Gonna leave me like you left me and mommy." Like Simz, Debelle traces this dynamic's impact on future romantic relationships. Vitally, London-born Debelle probes into conflicted feelings using a local accent. "We have a particular type of cadence, which is why things like grime just work so well for us," says Debelle.[6] "Our cadence is sharp," she continues, "we don't draw out our words in a way that North Americans do."[7] Early British rappers such as Cookie Crew did precisely this, losing what was distinct in their identity, until London Posse piloted the use of a London accent in hip-hop in the mid-'80s. In the early 2000s, Wiley developed this sensibility by assembling grime out of a mash-up of hip-hop and hardcore techno. This maturity in London-centric rap was vital when Simz hit her teens, as evidenced on the rapper's first mixtape, *Stratosphere* (2010). If the spoken word appears to address its subject more directly than a sung one, then accent enhances this by bringing lyrics even closer to speech. But "I Love You, I Hate You" owes much to other musical genres in addition to grime. "It's not to say that I'm not into grime or anything like that," Simz clarifies in 2017, after the release of her second LP, "[but] I just wanna be able to break the mold a bit and show people that there's many different sides to me."[8]

On *GREY Area*, Simz draws on neo-soul guest vocalists to handle the singing, including Michael Kiwanuka on "Flowers" and Cleo Sol on "Selfish." Two years later, Simz uses the same technique with *Sometimes I Might Be Introvert*, on which Sol also appears on "Woman." Two NPR Tiny Desk Concerts illuminate Simz's growing awareness of her vocal strengths. Where the first in 2017 features some uncertain singing, the second Tiny Desk Concert from 2021 shows an artist fully in control, with neo-soul guest vocalists singing and Simz focusing on spoken word. Backing vocalists repeat the central refrain in each chorus while Simz weaves around them. For "I Love You, I Hate You" to have emotive impact and function as a tainted love song, it's essential that Simz optimize her vocal approach.

The way the beat and backing track of "I Love You, I Hate You" provide a bed for the lyrics and voice is key. Central to this is Simz's collaboration with producer Inflo, leader of the music collective SAULT. "We really understand each other in the studio," enthuses Simz, "[and] he trusts my ear and I trust his."[9] On "I Love You, I Hate You" they create a backing track that sets an introductory orchestral flourish against a boom-bap beat. The blend of instrumentation and neo-soul backing vocals finds Simz polishing the rough edges of elements of hip-hop and grime until they are almost as smooth as mainstream pop.

"I Love You, I Hate You" ends with an orchestral flourish similar to how it started. Against it, Simz fires off the song's final verse, including the line "I'm not forgivin' for you, man, I'm forgivin' for me," with Simz turning the narrative back on itself, seeming to resolve the feelings of conflict. But then the bridge cues up the last chorus and with it, a reassertion of conflict: "And sometimes," before the backing vocalists repeat the chorus "I love you / I hate you."

1. Little Simz, quoted in Dhruva Balram, "Little Simz," *NME*, September 3, 2021, https://www.nme.com/big-reads/little-simz -cover-interview-2021-sometimes-i-might-be-introvert-3035532.

2. Simz, quoted in Balram, "Little Simz."

3. Simz, quoted in Balram, "Little Simz."

4. Little Simz, quoted in Jeff Ihaza, "Little Simz Gave It Everything She's Got, and It Shows," *Rolling Stone*, September 16, 2021, https://www.rollingstone.com/music/music-features/little-simz -introvert-interview-1223123/.

5. Little Simz, quoted in Simran Hans, "Rapper Little Simz: 'I Don't Hold Back—I Feel Super Free,'" *Guardian*, April 18, 2021, https://www.theguardian.com/music/2021/apr/18/rapper-little-simz -i-dont-hold-back-i-feel-super-free.

6. Speech Debelle, quoted in Arusa Qureshi, *Flip the Script: How Women Came to Rule Hip Hop* (Edinburgh: 404 Ink, 2021), 52–53.

7. Debelle, quoted in Qureshi, *Flip the Script*, 52–53.

8. Little Simz, quoted in Cyclone Wehner, "Why Little Simz Doesn't Wanna Be Boxed In as a Grime MC," *Music*, January 12, 2017, https://themusic.com.au/features/little-simz-cyclone /WQhKTUxPTnE/12-01-17.

9. Little Simz, quoted in Will Lavin, "Little Simz on Working with SAULT Producer Inflo: 'Our Chemistry Is Just Unmatched,'" *NME*, September 3, 2021, https://www.nme.com/news/music/little -simz-on-working-with-sault-producer-inflo-our-chemistry-is-just -unmatched-3036945.

Outro

The following songs are under consideration
for *Tainted Love 2*:

Nancy Sinatra and Lee Hazlewood,
"Summer Wine" (1966)
The Kinks, "Lola" (1970)
Kimiko Kasai, "Love for Sale" (1975)
Marvin Gaye, "Feel All My Love Inside" (1976)
Blondie, "Picture This" (1978)
Japan, "Nightporter" (1980)
Prince, "Sister" (1980)
Siouxsie and the Banshees, "Melt!" (1982)
ABC, "Poison Arrow" (1982)
Nas, "Undying Love" (1999)
Air, "Playground Love" (2000)
Goldfrapp, "Monster Love" (2008)
Tyler, the Creator, "She" (2011)
Lana del Rey, "Off to the Races" (2012)
St. Vincent, "Severed Crossed Fingers" (2014)
Baxter Dury, "Lips" (2014)
Dave, "Law of Attraction" (2021)

Acknowledgments

Parts of chapters were originally presented/published at EnsadLab, Paris; Design Academy Eindhoven; Camberwell College of Arts; V&A Dundee; the ADA Master's suite, and the Music, Media, Technology program at the University of Huddersfield; and *DAMN° Magazine*.

Thank you to Fraser Muggeridge for the design.

At Sternberg Press, thank you to Caroline Schneider for commissioning the book and Leah Whitman-Salkin for the incredible editing.

My thanks go to Simon Oliver for the special gift, Neil Arthur for the electrics, Frances Wallace for the ode to an American city, and Nick Simonin for murder.

The late Jonathan Lindley, whose own research while my PhD student, was a vital inspiration. Thank you.

Thank you to David Blamey, Adam Bradley of the RAP Lab at UCLA, Paulie Dale, Jeremy Deller, James Dyer, Gary Finnegan, Giulia, Dale Holmes, KL, Paul Morrish, Simon A. Morrison in the Department of Music at Princeton University, Rick Poynor, Steve Swindells, and Tom Wilcox for reading draft chapters. And for reading countless entire drafts and consistent wise counsel, thank you Sophie McKinlay and Rupert Howe.

Colophon

Alex Coles
Tainted Love
From Nina Simone to Kendrick Lamar

Published by Sternberg Press

Editor/Producer: Leah Whitman-Salkin
Proofreader: Anita Iannacchione
Design: Fraser Muggeridge and Manon Veyssière
Main typeface: Library by Pierre Pané-Farré
Additional typefaces: Portrait and Plantin
Inside cover: Fraser Muggeridge, *Bangladesh offset*, 2018
Printer: Tallinn Book Printers, Estonia

ISBN 978-3-95679-658-6

Distributed by The MIT Press, Art Data, Les presses du réel and Idea Books.

Sternberg Press
71–75 Sheldon Street
London WC2H 9JQ
www.sternberg-press.com

Sternberg Press

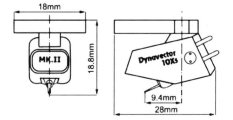

All vinyl played using a Dynavector cartridge.